DEVELOPMENTAL PROFILES
Pre-Birth Through Eight
2nd Edition

K. Eileen Allen
Lynn R. Marotz

DELMAR PUBLISHERS INC™
I(T)P™

NOTICE TO THE READER

Cover design by Kristina Almquist Design
Cover photo by Mike Gallitelli

Delmar Staff
Administrative Editor: Jay Whitney
Developmental Editor: Christopher Anzalone
Senior Project Editor: Andrea Edwards Myers
Production Coordinator: Sandra Woods
Art Design Coordinator: Doug Hyldelund

For information, address:

Delmar Publishers Inc.
3 Columbia Circle
P.O. Box 15-015
Albany, New York 12212-5015

COPYRIGHT © 1994
BY DELMAR PUBLISHERS INC

The trademark ITP is used under license.

Printed in the United States of America
Published simultaneously in Canada
by Nelson Canada,
a division of the Thomson Corporation

2 3 4 5 6 7 8 9 10 XXX 00 99 98 97 96 95 94

Library of Congress Cataloging-in-Publication Data
Allen, K. Eileen, 1918–
    Developmental profiled : pre-birth through eight / K. Eileen
Allen, Lynn R. Marotz. — 2nd ed.
      p.   cm.
    Rev. ed. of: Developmental profiles : birth to six. c1989.
    Includes index.
    ISBN 0-8273-5814-8
    1. Child development.   I. Marotz, Lynn R.   II. Title.
RJ131.A496   1994
155.4—dc20   93-45861
                                          CIP

Contents

Preface

Developmental Profiles: Pre-Birth through Eight, is a primer on child development designed for

- child development and early childhood students and teachers-in-training;
- child-care providers in home care settings, child care centers, preschools and Head Start Programs, and nannies in the child's own home;
- allied health professionals from fields such as nursing, nutrition, audiology, medicine, social work and physical therapy;
- parents, who are always the most important contributors to a child's optimum development.

The handbook contains non-technical, basic knowledge about

- what to expect of young children at each succeeding stage of development;
- the ways in which all areas of development are intertwined and mutually supportive;
- the unique pathway that each child follows in a developmental process that is alike, yet different, among children of similar age;
- the concept of developmental sequences being the crucial factor in development, not the child's chronological age;
- using development norms while performing observations and assessments.

This handbook offers a number of special features:

- concise profiles of developmental areas at various age levels from pre-birth through age eight;
- a section that briefly defines and describes the most commonly encountered terms and concepts in the child development literature;
- full color insert illustrating prenatal development;
- developmental alerts for each level, boxed separately for easy reference;
- descriptions of daily activities and routines typical of children at each level;
- where and how to get help if there is concern about a child's development;
- a comprehensive developmental checklist and growth charts to aid in the observation and screening process;
- sketches of infants, toddlers, the preschool child, and the school-age child;
- an annotated bibliography for back-up and additional readings on child development, screening and assessment, referral and information resources;
- appendices containing growth charts, reflex schedules, a sample health history form, and a number of other useful features.

Introduction

The second edition of *Developmental Profiles, Pre-Birth Through Eight* reflects changes and additions, however, the general format and nontechnical style remains the same: a comprehensive yet easy-to-read guide to early development. As before, the purpose of this primer is to supplement, rather than replace, a basic child development text. The goal continues to be that of supplying teachers, caregivers, and parents with readily accessible knowledge about the developing child—knowledge that will both enable and challenge these significant adults to provide warm and nurturing care, developmentally sound learning experiences, and appropriate guidance to every child, in every kind of setting.

CHANGES AND ADDITIONS

The scope of *Developmental Profiles* has been expanded to include a chapter on prenatal development and specific sections on six, seven, and eight-year-olds. The title of the book has been changed accordingly to *Developmental Profiles: Pre-Birth through Eight*.

EXTENSION TO SCHOOL-AGE CHILDREN

The inclusion of profiles of children of school age through grade three is in line with the current concensus of Early Childhood Educators. It is in line, too, with the position statement and curriculum manual published by the National Association for the Education of Young Children (NAEYC) which defines early childhood as including the eighth year. These age additions will conform with instructors' changing course outlines and also meet the needs of after school child care providers and those working in other capacities with six, seven, and eight-year-olds.

PRENATAL DEVELOPMENT

Because so much of a child's early development depends upon a good prenatal start, *Developmental Profiles* has been expanded to include a pre-birth chapter. The emphasis is on what takes place week-by-week and month-by-month in the developing fetus and what is needed to ensure its healthy development.

Additional emphasis has been placed on those developmental periods when the fetus is most susceptible to damage. Here the authors spell out principles of prevention beginning with the highly vulnerable early days and weeks of pregnancy.

LEARNING ACTIVITIES

A new boxed section entitled *Learning Activities* has been added to each unit immediately preceding *Developmental Alerts*. The boxes contain suggestions for appropriate activities and materials that adults can use to promote a variety of learning experiences at each age level. During the earliest days and months, the focus is on helping the infant learn to trust and interact with parents and caregiving adults. Later suggestions for adult-facilitated learning in young children emphasizes that everything a child needs to learn is learned best through unpressured play activities and frequent interactions with responsive adults.

REARRANGEMENT OF AGE DIVISIONS

A number of our readers suggested a regrouping of age divisions under the toddler heading. In response to these comments The Toddler now is divided simply by years—the one-year-old and the two-year-old.

PHILOSOPHICAL NOTES

To divide infancy and early childhood into specific units of months and years can distort the realities of ordinary development. Yet, when attempting to talk about developmental gains, delays, and expectations during the early years, no other format seems to work. Therefore, let it be stressed here, as it will be again and again in the test itself, the age specifications are only approximate markers derived from *averages* or *norms*. In a way, they can be thought of as midpoints intended to represent any one child. Age expectations also can be thought of as summary terms for skills that vary considerably from child to child in exact form and time of acquisition. The truly important consideration in assessing a child's development is *sequence*. The essential question is not chronological age but whether the child is moving forward step-by-step in each area of development. *Developmental Profiles* proves itself an invaluable resource in addressing this issue.

As in the first edition of *Developmental Profiles*, the early days, weeks, and months of infancy are looked at in great detail. This is how it should be. Research findings on infant development are truly astonishing—what the newborn, for example, is capable of learning is indeed amazing, especially in light of conventional wisdom implying that young babies simply flounder around in a kind of booming, buzzing confusion. Far from it! And so, with more and more infants entering infant programs at ever earlier ages, it is most important that caregivers are knowledgeable about infant development and infant learning and that parents can describe to caregivers what they want and believe best for their infants.

Certainly, the first year of life is critical in terms of foundation learnings in every area of development. Yet, the vast array of new and complex behaviors that toddlers and preschoolers must learn in three or four short years is also monumental. At no other period in a lifetime will so much be expected in so short a time. Again, with other-than-parent child care being the norm rather than the exception, it is essential that caregivers and parents have a thorough knowledge of how young children grow and develop and learn. Thus, an underlying theme of *Developmental Profiles* continues to be partnership with parents. No matter how many hours a day the child is with other caregivers, parents still play a most significant role. They need to be encouraged to talk about their child, their observations, their concerns. These bits of information are integral to the daily well-being of each child. And always, when parents talk, they need to be listened to with focused attention and responded to with genuine respect.

Partnership with parents becomes even more critical when an infant or child is suspected of having a developmental problem or irregularity. The Developmental Alerts following each age section can be especially useful to either a parent or teacher in initiating a discussion about their concerns. Let it be emphasized, however, that under no circumstances should this book or any other book be seen as an instrument for diagnosing a developmental problem. The purposes of this text can be summed up as follows:

- to provide easily accessible information about what to expect at each developmental level;
- to suggest appropriate ways for adults to facilitate learning and development during the early years;
- to pinpoint warning signs of a possible developmental problem;
- to suggest how and where to get help.

Acknowledgments

We are indebted to our editors at Delmar who have provided the encouragement and technical assistance to complete this project: Jay Whitney, Chris Anzalone, and Andrea Myers.

To our families for their patience and understanding. And, to our reviewers, a special thanks for their contributions: Mary Henthorne, Western Wisconsin Technical Center; Doris Usen, Erie Community College; P. Helen Lewis, Indiana University; Fran P. Kroll, Howard Community College; Roberta J. Hoyt, Duluth Vocational Center.

K. Eileen Allen, Professor Emeritus
University of Kansas
Lynn R. Marotz
University of Kansas

About the Authors

K. Eileen Allen retired as Professor Emeritus from the University of Kansas at Lawrence in 1987. While there, she taught both graduate and undergraduate courses in Human Development and Early Childhood Education and was a member of the Edna A. Hill Child Development Laboratory faculty. Upon retiring, she returned to her home in Seattle where she had taught at the University of Washington for nearly twenty years before taking the position at Kansas. Even after thirty years on the frontline of developmental research, laboratory school supervision, teacher training, and work with parents, she has yet to retire from professional life. She continues to write books and position papers, to critique research papers for major journals, and to serve as board member or consultant to several national and regional early childhood projects. Her textbooks continue to focus on early childhood education and development, on children with developmental problems, and on the interdisciplinary team approach to working with children and their families.

Lynn R. Marotz brings her nursing background and clinical experience with young children to the field of early childhood where her prime interests lie in teacher training, early recognition of health impairments and the promotion of wellness among young children. She joined the faculty of the Edna A. Hill Child Development Laboratory at the University of Kansas in 1977 and currently serves as the Health and Safety Coordinator and Associate Director. She teaches a variety of courses and works closely with graduate and undergraduate students in the early-childhood teacher-training program. Her experience also includes extensive involvement with health screenings, communicating and working with parents and health professionals, and the referral process. Lynn Marotz has made numerous presentations and authored publications on a variety of issues related to children's health, identification of illness and developmental conditions, environmental safety, and nutrition.

CHAPTER 1

Principal Concepts in Child Development

To provide effective care and guidance for young children, it is essential to understand the principal concepts of child development. Each child's overall development and behavior can then be put into focus, day by day. Such understanding also gives a long-range perspective on each child. This two-track approach is indispensible in helping all children grow and develop in ways best-suited to each as an unique individual.

The following key concepts have been selected because of their current importance and widespread use in the field of child development. Varied as these concepts are, it is necessary to understand and apply all of them in working effectively with infants and young children.

BASIC NEEDS

All children, whether normal, handicapped or **at-risk** for developmental problems, have a number of physical and psychological needs. These needs must be met if infants and children are to survive, thrive, and develop to their optimum potential. Many developmental psychologists view the early years as the most critical in the entire developmental lifespan. Never again will the child be so totally dependent upon parents, caregivers, and teachers to satisfy the basic needs of life and to provide opportunities for learning.

Although separated in the lists that follow, it must be understood that physical and psychological needs are interrelated and interdependent. Meeting a child's physical needs while neglecting psychological needs may lead to developmental problems. The opposite also is true—a child who is physically neglected frequently experiences trouble in learning and getting along with others.

at-risk—Describes children who may be more likely to have developmental problems due to certain predisposing factors.

Children need affection.

Basic physical needs

- Shelter, protection from harm.
- Food, nutritious and appropriate to age of child.
- Warmth, adequate clothing.
- Preventive health, and dental care; treatment of physical and mental conditions.
- Cleanliness.
- Rest and activity, in balance.

Psychological Needs

- Affection and consistency—**nurturing** parents and caregivers who can be depended upon to be there for the child.
- Security and trust—familiar surroundings with parents and caregivers who respond reliably and appropriately to the needs of the infant and child.
- Appropriate adult expectations as to what the child can and cannot do at each level of development.

The Need to Learn

- Freedom to explore and experiment with necessary limits clearly stated and consistently maintained.
- Access to developmentally appropriate experiences and play materials.

---

nurturing—*Nurturing includes qualities of warmth, loving, caring, and attention to physical needs.*

Children need freedom to explore.

- An appropriate "match" between a child's skill levels and the materials and experiences available to the child: just enough newness to challenge, but not so much that the child feels overwhelmed, incapable or excessively frustrated.
- Errors, mistakes and failures treated as important steps in the learning process, never as reasons for condemning or ridiculing a child.
- Adults who demonstrate in everyday life the appropriate behaviors expected of the child, be it language, social interactions or ways of handling stress. *Remember: parents, caregivers, and teachers are major models of behavior for young children.*

The Need for Respect

- A respectful and helpful environment in which the child's efforts are encouraged, approved and aided: "You picked up your crayons. Good job. Shall I put them on the shelf for you?"
- Acceptance of the child's efforts; respect for accomplishments whether small or large, for errors as well as successes: "Look at that! You laced your shoes all by yourself." (No mention of the eyelet that was missed.)
- Recognition that accomplishment, the "I can do it" attitude, is the major and most essential component of a child's **self-esteem**: "You're really getting good at cutting out cookies."
- Sincere attention to what the child is doing well; using descriptive praise to help children learn to recognize and respect their accomplishments: "You got your shoes on the right feet all by yourself."

---

self-esteem—Feelings about one's self-worth.

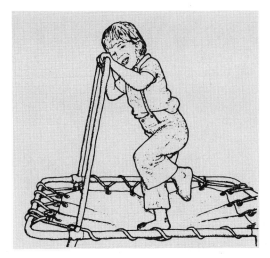

Children need respect for accomplishments.

New skills are built on previously learned skills.

- Awareness of the tremendous amount of effort and concentration that goes into acquiring developmental skills; positive responses to each small step along the way as a child works toward mastery of a complex skill such as self-feeding with a spoon. "Right! Just a little applesauce on the spoon so it stays on."

NORMAL DEVELOPMENT

The term "normal development" is used in many different ways and is difficult to define simply and specifically. In general, it implies that a child is growing, changing and acquiring a broad range of skills according to some unobservable inner pattern or timetable. However, such a statement oversimplifies the concept of normal development. Several additional factors must be considered. Development also involves the following:

- An integrated process by which children change in orderly ways in terms of size, **neurological** structure and behavioral complexity;
- A cumulative or "building block" process; each new aspect of growth or development includes and builds upon earlier changes; each new behavioral or physical accomplishment is necessary to the next stage or next set of skills;

---

neurological—Refers to the brain and nervous system.

Learning through experience.

- A continuous process of give and take between the child and the environment, each changing the other in a variety of ways. (For example: The three-year-old drops a cup, breaks it, and the parent scolds the child. Both events, the broken cup and parent's displeasure, are environmental changes that the child has created. From this experience the child learns to hold on more firmly next time, and this constitutes a change in the child's behavior—fewer broken cups.)

A number of other key concepts also are closely related to the basic concept of normal development. These will be touched upon one by one.

Developmental Milestones
Developmental milestones are major markers or points of accomplishment in children's development. They are made up of important motor, social, cognitive, and language skills. They show up in somewhat orderly steps and within fairly predictable age ranges. Essentially, milestone behaviors are those that most normally developing children are likely to display at approximately the same age. For example, almost every child begins to smile between four and ten weeks, speak a first word or two around twelve months. These achievements (social smile, first words) are but two of a number of highly significant behavioral indications that a child's developmental progress is on track. The failure of one or more developmental milestones to appear within a reasonable range of time is a warning that a child should be observed closely.

Sequences of Development
A sequence or pattern of development consists of predictable steps along a developmental pathway common to the majority of children. Children must be able to roll over before they can sit and sit before they can stand. *The critical*

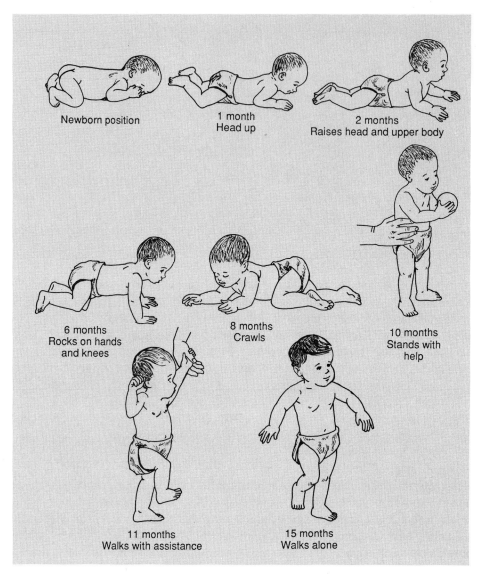

Sequence of motor development.

consideration is the order in which children acquire these developmental skills, not their age in months and years. The appropriate sequence of development is an important indication that the child is moving steadily forward along a sound developmental **continuum**. In language development, for example, it does not matter how many words a child speaks by two years of age. What is important is that

---

continuum—A continuous pathway.

the child has progressed from cooing and babbling to "jabbering" (inflected jargon), to syllable production. The two-year-old who has progressed through those stages usually produces words and sentences within a reasonable period of time.

Developmental progress is rarely smooth and even. Irregularities, such as periods of **stammering** or a **food jag**, characterize development. Regression, that is taking a step or two backward now and again, is perfectly normal and is to be expected: a child who has been toilet trained may begin to have "accidents" when starting preschool or child care.

Age-Level Expectancies or Norms

Age-level expectancies can be thought of as chronological or age-related levels of development. Investigators like Gesell, Bailey, and Frankenburg carried out systematic observations on vast numbers of infants and children of various ages. Analyses of their findings represent the average or "normal" age at which many specifically described developmental skills are acquired by most children in a given culture. This average age is often called the norm; thus a child's development may be described as at the norm, above the norm or below the norm. For example, a child who walks at 8 1/2 months is ahead of the norm at 12 to 15 months, while a child who does not walk until 20 months is behind the norm.

One point must be stressed: age-level expectancies *always represent a range and never an exact point in time* when specific skills will be achieved. Profiles of age expectancies for specific skills always should be interpreted as approximate midpoints on a range of months (as in the example walking, from 8 to 20 months with the midpoint at 14 months.) Once again, a reminder: it is *sequence* and *not age* that is the important factor in evaluating a child's progress.

Range of Normalcy

In real life, there is probably no child who is truly normal in every way. The range of skills and the age at which skills are acquired show great variation. This is true even among children who are described as being typical or as developing normally. Relevant again is the example of walking, one infant starting at 8 1/2 months and another not until 20 months. Both are within the normal range, though many months apart on either side of the norm. No two children grow and develop at exactly the same rate, nor do they perform in exactly the same way. There are a half-dozen perfectly normal ways of creeping and crawling. Most children, however, use what is referred to as contralateral locomotion, an

---

stammering—To speak in an interrupted or repetitive pattern.

food jag—A period when only certain foods are preferred or accepted.

**Behavior problems are not uncommon
during transitions and consolidations.**

opposite knee-hand method of getting about, prior to walking. Also, some normally walking two-year-olds have never crawled. Thus, normalcy encompasses great variation and a wide range of differences among individual children.

Developmental Transitions and Consolidations

Development can be thought of as a series of phases. Spurts of rapid growth and development often are followed by periods of disorganization. Then the child seems to recover and move into a period of reorganization. It is not at all uncommon for children to demonstrate behavior problems or even regression during these periods. The reasons vary. Perhaps the new baby has become an active and engaging older infant who is now the center of family attention. Three-year-old brother may revert to babyish ways about the same time. He begins to have tantrums over minor frustrations, and may, for the time being, lose his hard-won bladder control. Usually, these transition periods are short-lived. The three-year-old, for example, will almost always learn more age-appropriate ways of getting attention given adult support and understanding.

Interrelatedness of Developmental Areas

As noted in the beginning, discussions about development usually are divided into five major areas: physical, motor, perceptual, cognitive, personal-social, and language. However, no single area develops independently of other developmental areas. Every skill, whether simple or complex, is a mixture. Social skills are an example. Why are some young children said to have good social skills? Often the answer is because they play well with other children and are sought as playmates. But to be a preferred playmate, a child must have many skills. A four-year-old, for example, should be able to:

- Run, jump, climb, and build with blocks (good motor skills);
- Ask for, explain, and describe what is going on (good language skills);
- Recognize likenesses and differences among play materials and so select the right materials in a joint building project (good perceptual skills);
- Problem solve, conceptualize and plan ahead in cooperative play ventures (good cognitive skills).

Every developmental area is well-represented in the above example, even though social development was the primary area under consideration.

Heredity and Environment (The Nature/Nurture Controversy)

Each child has a unique **genetic** makeup. Genetic makeup influences a child's temperament, energy level, and rate of physical and intellectual development. However, no aspect of a child's makeup, except perhaps eye color, hair color, shape of nose and certain other physical characteristics, can be attributed exclusively to heredity (internal influences) or to environment (external influences). From the moment of conception, environmental factors continuously interact and contribute to the child's genetic pattern of growth and development.

Maturation

Maturation implies changes that are primarily biological: it is the appearance of new skills or behaviors common to all developing human beings. Sitting, walking and talking are examples or maturation. As noted earlier, these skills do not come about independently of the environment. Learning to walk, for example, involves muscle strength and coordination (influenced by adequate nutrition). Learning to walk also requires an environment that encourages practice, not only of walking as it emerges, but also of the behaviors and skills that preceded walking, such as rolling over, sitting, and crawling.

Individual Differences

A number of factors contribute to making each child unique, special, or different from every other child. Genetic inheritance and environment have been discussed. Several additional factors will be touched upon next.

Temperament. Temperament refers to an individual's patterns of behaviors or responses to everyday happenings. Infants and young children differ in their activity level, alertness, irritability, soothability, restlessness and cuddliness. Such qualities often lead to labels—the "easy" child, the "difficult" child, the "slow to warm-up" child. These characteristics (and labels) seem to have a definite effect on the ways that family, caregivers and teachers respond to the child. This, in turn, reinforces the child's self-perceptions. For example, a slow-to-warm-up

---

genetic—Refers to inherited biological qualities.

**Cultural and economic factors influence
development before birth.**

child is often treated with hostility by others. This treatment, in turn, tends to justify to the child his or her hostile behaviors.

Sex Roles. Early in life, young children learn the sex roles that are considered appropriate by their culture. Each boy and girl develops a set of behaviors, attitudes and commitments that are defined for them, directly or indirectly, as being acceptable male or female behaviors. In addition, each child plays out sex roles according to everyday experiences. In other words, each child's sex role development will be influenced by playmates and play opportunities, toys, type and amount of television, and especially by adult models (parents, neighbors, teachers).

Culture and Economic Factors. Long before birth, cultural and economic factors influence the child's uniqueness. These influences include the following:

- General health and nutrition of the mother
- The mother's understanding of her obligations and responsibilities to her unborn child
- Availability of pre- and post-natal medical care
- Ethnic and religious beliefs and practices

Factors such as these contribute to each child being unlike any other child. For example, the child born to a single, fifteen-year-old parent living in poverty will be different from a child born and raised in a two-parent, professional family.

Transactional Patterns of Development
From birth, the child begins to influence the behavior of parents and caregivers. In turn, parents and caregivers influence the child. Thus, development is a give-

and-take process in which parents, caregivers, teachers, and the child are continuously interacting in ways that influence each other's behaviors.   For example, a calm, cuddly baby expresses its needs in a clear and predictable fashion.   This infant begins life with personal-social experiences that are quite different from those of a tense, colicky infant whose sleeping and eating patterns are highly irregular and, therefore, stressful to parents. The transactional process between infants and parents will be quite different in each instance and so will the developmental outcome.

Contingent Stimulation

This term refers to the specific ways in which parents and caregivers respond to a child's efforts to get attention. Children thrive when adults respond promptly and positively, at least a fair share of the time, to appropriate things a child says and does. Developmental research indicates that children develop healthier self-concepts, as well as earlier and better language, cognitive and social skills if raised with responsive adults.   Contingent stimulation, therefore, must not be overlooked as a major factor in facilitating a child's progress in all areas of development.

ATYPICAL DEVELOPMENT

The term atypical is used to describe children with developmental problems—children whose development appears to be incomplete or inconsistent with normal patterns and sequences. These children are often said to be either delayed or different in their development, perhaps even handicapped. The child with developmental delays can be described as one who is performing in one or more areas of development like a much younger, normal child. The child who is still babbling with no recognizable words at age three is an example of delayed development. This condition need not be handicapping unless the child never develops **functional language**. Developmental deviation refers to an aspect of development that is different from what is ever seen in a normally developing child.   The child born with six toes or with a profound hearing loss has a developmental deviation.   The six-toed child is not likely to be considered handicapped while the deaf child may have a serious and, perhaps, life-long handicap. In any event, the concepts and principles described on the foregoing pages apply to the child with developmental problems, as well as the child who is said to be developing normally.

In conclusion, this brief discussion of significant principles and concepts related to child development is intended to refresh, enhance and update the readers'

---

functional language—Language that allows children to get what they need or want.

understanding of the developing child. The developmental profiles that follow will have greater meaning and value when used in the context of these basic principles and concepts.

REVIEW QUESTIONS

1. List three psychological needs of the developing child.
   a.

   b.

   c.

2. List three terms related to normal developmental progression.
   a.

   b.

   c.

3. List three ways in which an adult can show respect for a young child's accomplishments.
   a.

   b.

   c.

TRUE OR FALSE

1. All that a child needs to develop fully is adequate food, warm housing, adequate clothing and good medical attention.

2. Errors, mistakes and failures displayed by a young child provide opportunities for learning.

3. Each new accomplishment in a young child's development is built upon earlier skills and experiences.

4. Environment has very little effect on a child's long-term development.

5. Maturation is biologically based (for the most part) and includes such things as learning to sit up, crawl, and walk.

6. The child with developmental delays is handicapped throughout life.

MULTIPLE CHOICE. Select one or more correct answers from the lists below.

1. All areas of development are
    a. interrelated.
    b. interdependent.
    c. influenced by environment.

2. Development is
    a. cumulative, a building-block process.
    b. independent of neurological structure.
    c. physically and psychologically interactive.

3. Most normally developing children
    a. begin to smile between four and ten weeks.
    b. walk no later than one year.
    c. are talking in sentences by two years of age.

4. Development can be thought of as a series of phases that
    a. all children go through at the same age.
    b. show no regression; the child always goes forward, never backwards.
    c. are influenced by economic and cultural factors.

5. Children develop healthier self concepts when adults provide
    a. contingent stimulation.
    b. frequent criticism and disapproval of errors the child makes.
    c. ample praise, especially descriptive praise.

CHAPTER 2

Growth and Development

BASIC CONCEPTS

Growth and development are terms often used interchangeably. Yet, they are not identical concepts. Each refers to distinct aspects of the life process.

Growth refers to specific changes and increases in the child's actual size. Additional numbers of cells, as well as an increase in the size of existing cells, account for the observable increases in a child's height, weight, head circumference, shoe size, length of arms and legs, and body shape. All growth changes lend themselves to direct and fairly reliable measurement.

The growth process is continuous throughout the child's life span. However, the rate of growth varies considerably according to age. For example, growth occurs

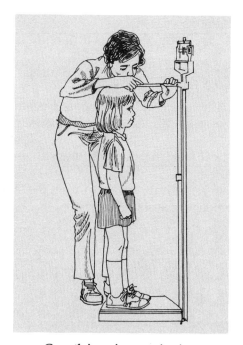

Growth is an increase in size.

14 .

rapidly during infancy and adolescence. In contrast, growth is slower and less dramatic in the preschool-age child and in the adult. Yet even when the child reaches adulthood, the body continues to repair and replace its cells.

Development refers to an increase in complexity, a change from relatively simple to more complicated. It involves an orderly progression along a continuous pathway on which the child acquires more refined knowledge, behaviors, and skills. The sequence is basically the same for all children. However, the rate of development varies from child to child (see Chapter 1).

A child's rate and level of development are closely related to physiological maturity, especially of the nervous and muscular systems. Also, development is influenced by biological makeup (heredity) and environmental factors that are unique to each individual. Together, these factors account for the range of variations in individual children's development.

Normal growth and development is a term used to indicate **acquisition** of certain skills and behaviors according to a predictable rate and sequence. As noted in Chapter 1, the range of what is considered normal is broad. It includes mild variations and simple irregularities: the three-year-old who lisps, the twelve-month-old who learns to walk without having crawled.

At-risk is a phrase used to describe infants and young children who have a high probability of developing problems: newborns who were premature and of low-birth weight; infants whose mothers had poor nutrition; children of teenage parents. Early identification and intervention are of crucial importance with infants and children at-risk for developmental problems.

The term *atypical* is used to describe a child's growth or development that is incomplete or inconsistent with the normal sequence. Abnormal development in one area may or may not interfere with the development and mastery of skills in other areas. There are many reasons for atypical development including genetic abnormalities, poor nutrition, illness, injury, and lack of opportunities to learn.

DEVELOPMENTAL AREAS

To describe and accurately assess children's developmental progress, it is necessary to have a framework within which to work. For discussion purposes in this textbook, six major developmental areas have been identified: growth and physical development; motor; perceptual; cognitive; speech and language;

---

acquisition—The process of learning or achieving specific objectives.

personal-social. Each area includes many kinds of skills and behaviors, which will be discussed in the developmental profiles that follow. Although these developmental areas, as noted earlier, are separated for the purpose of discussion, they cannot be separated from one another in reality. Each is integrally related to, and interdependent with, each of the others.

Developmental profiles or "word pictures" are useful for assessing the current and on-going status of children's skills and behavior. Keep in mind that the rate of development is uneven and occasionally unpredictable across areas, especially during the first two years of a child's life. For example, the language and social skills of infants and toddlers are less well-developed than their ability to move about. Also, children's individual achievements may vary across developmental areas: a child may walk late, but talk early. Again, an important reminder: development in any of the areas is dependent on children having appropriate stimulation and opportunities to learn.

Physical development and growth are the major tasks of early infancy and child-hood. Governed by heredity and greatly influenced by environmental condi-tions, physical development and growth is a highly individualized process. It is responsible for changes in body shape and proportions as well as overall body size. Growth, and especially growth of the brain, occurs more rapidly during prenatal development and the first year than at any other time. Growth is intricately related to progress in other developmental areas, too. It results in increased muscle strength for movement, depth perception in reaching for objects, and improved muscular control for bladder training. The state of a child's physical development serves as a reliable index of general health and well-being. It also has a direct influence on determining whether children are likely to achieve their potential in each of the other developmental areas, including intellectual achievement.

Motor development refers to a child's ability to move about and control various body parts. Refinements in motor development depend on maturation of the brain, input from the sensory system, increased bulk and number of muscle fibers, a healthy nervous system, and opportunities to practice.

Motor abilities during early infancy are purely **reflexive**; most gradually dis-appear as the child develops voluntary control. If these earliest reflexes do not phase out at appropriate times in the developmental sequence, it may be an

---

reflexive—Acts or movements resulting from impulses of the nervous system that cannot be controlled by the individual are reflexive.

voluntary—Movements that can be willed and purposively controlled and initiated by the individual are voluntary.

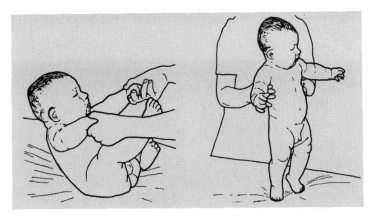

Cephalo-caudal development proceeds from head to toe.

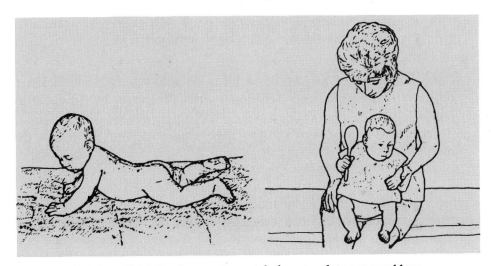

Proximo-distal development proceeds from trunk to arms and legs.

indication of neurological problems (see Appendix 1). In such cases, medical evaluation should be sought.

Three principles govern motor development:

1. *Cephalo-caudal*: muscular development that proceeds from head to toe. The infant first learns to control muscles that support first the head and neck, then the trunk, and later those that allow reaching. Muscles for walking develop last.
2. *Proximo-distal*: muscular development that begins with improved control of muscles closest to the central portion of the body, gradually moving outward and away from the midpoint to the extremities (arms and legs).

Refinement means the fine-tuning of a skill.

Control of the head and neck is achieved before the child can pick up an object with thumb and forefinger (pincer grasp or finger-thumb opposition).

3. *Refinement*: muscular development that progresses from general or **gross motor** control used in sitting up or walking, to specific fine motor control, such as feeding self with a spoon.

Perceptual development refers to the increasingly complex use the child makes of information received through the senses: sight, hearing, touch, smell, taste, and body position. In one sense, perception is concerned with how any one or any combinations of the senses are used. Perception also involves learning to select specific aspects of the environment on which to focus. In other words, which details of a situation are important? Which differences should be noted? Which should be ignored? Even these simple questions demonstrate how difficult, if not impossible, it is to separate perceptual from cognitive processes. Separating these processes is a problem that occurred again and again in preparing the profiles that follow; thus, a decision to combine perception and cognition.

Three aspects of perceptual development will be addressed:

1. *Multi-modality*: Information is generally received through more than one sense organ at a time; when listening to a speaker, we use sight (watching facial expressions and gestures) and sound (listening to the words).

---

gross motor—Gross motor skills involve large muscle movements: walking, running, reaching.

Multi-modality means the child uses
information gathered by many senses.

Habituation

2. *Habituation*: This is the ability to ignore everything except what is most important to the immediate situation; the child who is unaware of a telephone conversation in the background and focuses, instead, on the story being read.

3. *Sensory integration*: The child translates **sensory information** into intelligent behavior; the five-year-old sees and hears a truck coming and waits on the curb for it to pass.

Rudiments of the perceptual system are in place at the time of birth. Through experience, learning, and maturation it develops into a smoothly coordinated operation for processing complex information (sorting shapes according to size and color) and making fine discriminations (telling the difference among initial sounds in rhyming words, such as rake, cake, lake). The sensory system also enables an individual to respond appropriately to all kinds of messages and signals: smiling in response to a smile; keeping quiet in response to a frown.

Cognitive development has to do with the expansion of a child's intellect or mental abilities. Cognition is finding, processing, and organizing information and then using the information appropriately. The cognitive process includes such mental activities as discovering, interpreting, sorting, classifying, and remembering information. In older children it means evaluating ideas, making judgments,

---

***sensory information**—Information received through the senses: eyes, ears, nose, mouth, touch.*

Sensory integration

solving problems, understanding rules and concepts, thinking ahead and visualizing possibilities or consequences. Cognitive development is an ongoing process of interaction between the child and objects or events in the environment.

Cognitive development begins with the reflexive behaviors that permit survival and primitive learning in the newborn. Next comes what Piaget has labelled the stage of sensory-motor activity. This stage lasts until approximately age two. The sensory-motor period is followed by a time of preoperational activity (another Piagetian term) that allows young children to internally process information coming in through their senses. Again it must be stressed that it is difficult, if not impossible, to discuss cognition as a separate developmental area, especially in the earliest years. Always there is overlap with both perceptual development and motor involvement. As the child matures, a further complication comes about—the overlap with language development.

Language Development Language is often defined as a system of symbols, both spoken and written. It is a system that allows humans to communicate with one another. Normal *language development* is regular and sequential. It depends upon maturation as well as learning opportunities. The first year of life is called the prelinguistic or prelanguage phase. This is followed by the linguistic or language stage where speech becomes the major way of communicating. Words and grammatical rules are acquired as children gain skill in conveying their thoughts and ideas through language.

In terms of speech and language development, children seem to understand concepts and relationships long before they have the words to describe them. In other words, receptive language (understanding what is said) precedes expressive language (the ability to use words to describe and explain). Speech and language development depend on, and are related to, the child's general cognitive development. However, language development also depends on the type of language the child hears and maturation of the neuromuscular system.

Personal and social development is a broad area that concerns how children feel about themselves and their relationships with others. It refers to children's individual behaviors and responses to play and work activities, attachments to parents and caregivers and relationships with brothers, sisters, and friends. Sex roles, independence, morality, trust, accepting rules and laws—these, too, are basic aspects of personal and social development. The family and its cultural values are influential factors in shaping a child's social development and determining much of a child's basic personality.

In describing personal and social development, it must be remembered once again that children develop at different rates. Individual differences in genetic endowment, cultural background, health status, and a host of other environmental factors, such as experiences in child care, contribute to these variations. Therefore, no two children can ever be exactly alike, not in social development or in any other area of development.

AGE DIVISIONS

The age divisions throughout this book are common to those used by many child developmentalists when describing significant changes within developmental areas:

Infant—	0–28 days (neonate, newborn)
	1–4 months
	4–8 months
	8–12 months
Toddler—	12–24 months
	24–36 months
Preschool—	3–5 years
Six and Beyond—	6–8 years

Age divisions are to be used with extreme caution and great flexibility when dealing with real children. They are based on the averaged achievements, abilities, and behaviors of many children at various stages in development. As has been stated again and again, there is great variation from one child to another, and *it is sequence, not age*, that is the major index to development.

In conclusion, this chapter provides a review of terms commonly used to describe the major developmental areas. These concepts are the foundation upon which the profiles were developed. It is important that everyone working with young children understand the concepts and their many variations in order to use the developmental profiles effectively.

REVIEW QUESTIONS

1. List three factors related to a child's rate of development.
   a.

   b.

   c.

2. List three factors that may lead to atypical or abnormal development.
   a.

   b.

   c.

3. List three sources of perceptual information.
   a.

   b.

   c.

TRUE OR FALSE

1. The terms growth and development can be used interchangeably because they mean exactly the same thing.

2. The rate at which a child develops is identical to all other children of the same age and sex.

3. Premature infants are often at-risk for developmental problems.

4. Malnutrition during the mother's pregnancy can have a damaging effect on the child's development after it is born.

5. Growth of the brain occurs most rapidly during the latter part of the prenatal period and the infant's first year of life.

6. Perceptual development depends upon what the infant sees, hears, smells, tastes and touches.

7. The entire perceptual system is in place at the time of birth.

8. Receptive language develops after expressive language.

MULTIPLE CHOICE. Select one or more correct answers from the lists below.

1. Development is
   a. a change from simple to complex skills.
   b. a sequential process that is basically the same for all children.
   c. variable in terms of rate—that is, some children may walk earlier than others but talk later and still be considered normal.

2. Motor development during early infancy
   a. is almost entirely reflexive.
   b. is not associated with cognitive development.
   c. can be speeded up with direct teaching and practice.

3. Which of the following terms are associated predominantly with motor development?
   a. sensory integration
   b. proximo-distal
   c. cephalo-caudal

4. Which of the following terms are important to perceptual development?
   a. sensory integration
   b. racial integration
   c. school integration

5 . Personal and social development are influenced by
   a. heredity.
   b. general health.
   c. culture and race.

6. Growth is
    a. measurable.
    b. faster during the preschool years than during infancy.
    c. continuous, in one form or another, throughout most of life.

PREBIRTH DEVELOPMENT

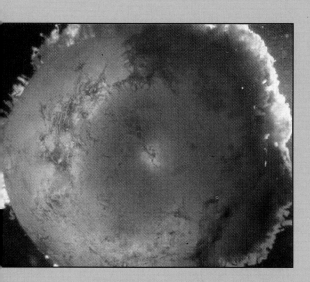

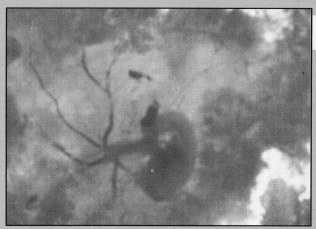

There are approximately 266 days of prebirth development. During the germinal stage (first 14 days) the sperm merges with the ovum forming a zygote which attaches itself to the mother's uterus.

During the embryonic stage (14–56 days) the development of the fetus is critical. It is at this stage that specialized cells will begin to form the major organs and systems including the heart, lungs, and brain.

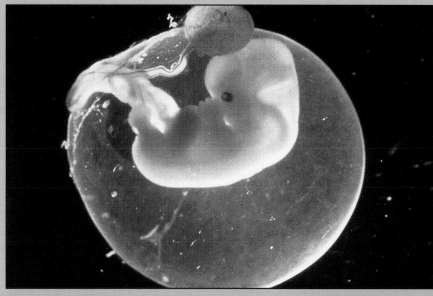

During the embryonic stage, the fetus is extremely vulnerable to any chemical sub-stances and infectious diseases the mother may be exposed to.

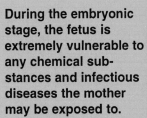

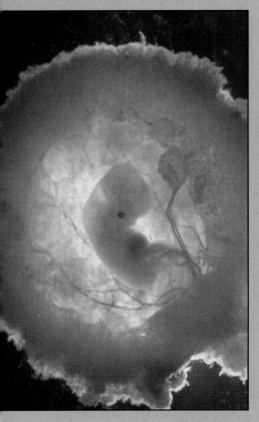

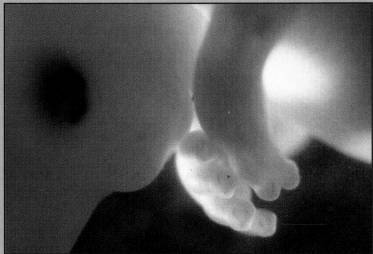

In the second month of pregnancy, the eyes, ears, nasal organs, and jaw form. The heart is divided into four chambers. The tail-like appendage begins to regress.

The fetal period begins about the ninth week and ends at birth. The finger-nails, toenails, and hair follicles form. The head becomes proportional to the rest of the body.

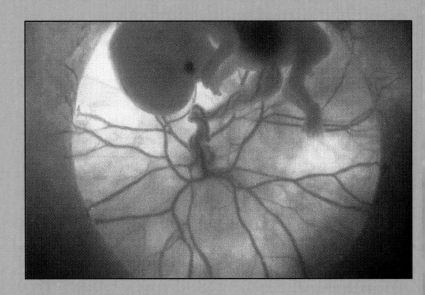

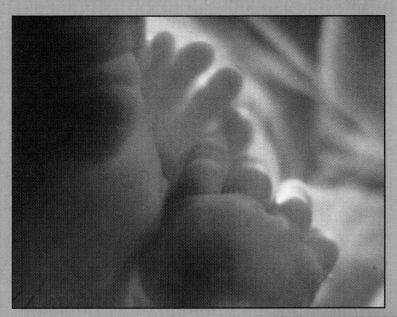

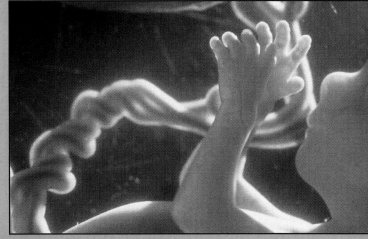

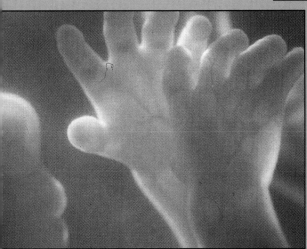

Between the fourth and seventh month, the fetus can see, hear, and produce crying sounds. The heartbeat can be heard through the mother's abdomen and the lungs are sufficiently developed to be used at birth.

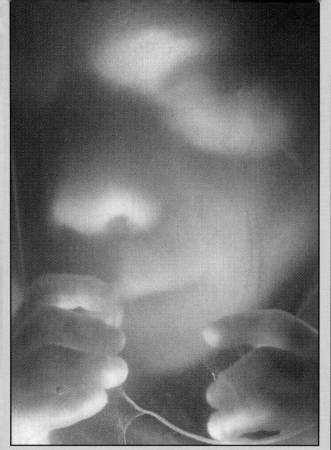

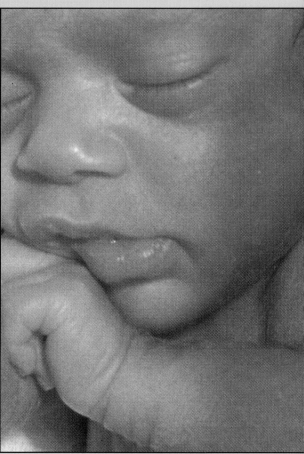

During the final eight weeks of pregnancy, the fetus adds about half its total weight and drops down into the mother's pelvis, ready for birth.

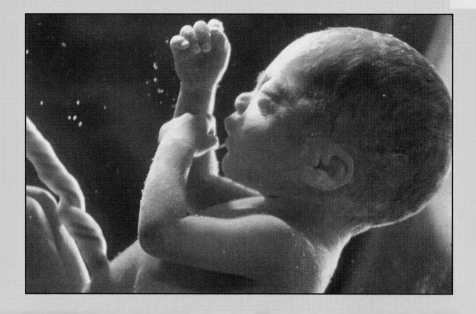

CHAPTER 3

Prenatal Development

Each of the approximately 266 days of prenatal development (from **conception** to birth) is critical to producing a healthy newborn. Fairly, or unfairly, the major responsibility for healthy fetal development lies with the mother. She is the source of everything the **in utero** infant requires if it is to be born ready and able to cope with life "on the outside." The infant does inherit **genes** from its father; these will determine certain physical characteristics and, perhaps, traits of temperament. Also, the development of the unborn infant can be enhanced when the father provides caring support for the mother throughout pregnancy. Nevertheless, it is the mother, because she is the provider of everything physically essential (and harmful) to fetal development, who plays the major role in producing a healthy baby. Therefore, it is important that patterns of normal prenatal development, as well as practices that both promote and interfere with this process, are clearly understood by every parent.

THE DEVELOPMENT PROCESS

The prenatal period is commonly divided into stages. In obstetrical practice, pregnancy is classified according to trimesters, each consisting of three calendar months:

- first trimester—conception through the third month
- second trimester—fourth through the sixth month
- third trimester—seventh through the ninth month

Pregnancy also may be discussed in terms of fetal development. This approach emphasizes critical changes that occur week by week. It, too, encompasses three stages:

---

conception—The joining of a single egg or ovum from the female and a single sperm from the male.

in utero—The period when the infant is developing within the mother's uterus.

genes—Genetic material that carries codes, or information, for all inherited characteristics.

Germinal stage refers to the first fourteen days of pregnancy. The merging of an ovum and sperm produces a zygote. Cell division begins and forms a pinhead-sized mass of specialized cells called a blastocyst. This small mass attaches itself to the wall of the mother's uterus. Successful attachment (**implantation**) marks the start of the **embryo** and the embryonic stage.

Embryonic stage includes the fourteenth day through the eighth week. This stage is critical to the overall development of the fetus. Continuing cell division results in specialized cell layers that gradually form major organs and systems, such as the heart, lungs, and brain. Many of these structures will be functional near the end of this period. Embryonic blood, for example, begins to flow through the fetus' primitive cardiovascular system (heart and blood vessels) in the fourth to the fifth week.

During this time, other important changes are taking place. Once implantation is completed, a placenta begins to form. It serves four major purposes:

- To supply nutrients and hormones to the fetus.
- To remove fetal waste products throughout the pregnancy.
- To filter out many harmful substances, as well as viruses and other disease-causing organisms. (Unfortunately, many drugs get through the placenta's filtering system.)
- To act as a temporary immune system by supplying the fetus with the same antibodies the mother produces against certain infectious diseases. (In most instances, the infant is protected for approximately six months following birth.)

As the placenta is forming, an umbilical cord also develops. This cord establishes linkage between the fetus, its mother, and her health and general lifestyle. At this point, the fetus is highly vulnerable to chemical substances and infectious diseases that enter the mother's body. These factors can cause serious damage to the fetus' major organs and systems, which are being formed at this time. As we will see in a later section, the result may be irreversible birth defects, ranging from mild to severe.

Fetal stage refers to the ninth week of pregnancy until birth (generally the thirty-eighth week). Most systems and structures are now formed and so, this last and longest period is devoted to growth and maturity. By the twelfth week, eyelids,

---

implantation—The attachment of the blastocyst to the wall of the mother's uterus; occurs around the twelfth day.

embryo—Describes the cell mass from the time of implantation through the eighth week of pregnancy.

lips, fingers, and toes are present and gender can be determined. Around the sixteenth week, the mother begins to feel the fetus moving. By the twenty-eighth week, the breathing, blood, and nervous systems are sufficiently developed that the infant can survive if born prematurely. During the final two months, few developmental changes occur. Instead, there are rapid and important gains in weight and size: a seven–month–old fetus weighs approximately three pounds (3.2 kg). Body systems are also strengthening and maturing so the fetus can maintain itself outside the mother's body. Refer to the color insert which illustrates the stages of prenatal development.

PROMOTING OPTIMUM FETAL DEVELOPMENT

Critical aspects of development are taking place in the earliest days of pregnancy, often before it has even been confirmed. Therefore, it is important that both mother and father practice healthy lifestyles throughout their reproductive years. Research provides essential information about the many factors that improve a mother's chances of having a healthy baby. These include:

- professional prenatal care
- good nutrition
- sufficient rest
- moderate weight gain
- regular exercise
- positive emotional state
- mother's age and general health

Prenatal Care
Medically supervised prenatal care is critical for ensuring the development of a healthy baby. Arrangements for such care should be made as soon as a woman suspects that she is pregnant. During the initial visit to a health care provider, pregnancy can be confirmed (or refuted), and any medical problems the mother may have can be evaluated and treated. During subsequent visits, the pregnant woman can be advised about factors that influence fetal development. For example, mothers might be encouraged to participate in regular, non-contact exercise. (As long as there are no limiting complications, regular exercise helps with weight control, increases muscle tone, and is believed to contribute to easier labor and delivery.)

Nutrition
The mother's nutritional status, determined by what she eats before and during pregnancy, has a significant effect on her own health, as well as on that of the developing fetus. Good maternal nutrition helps to prevent premature birth and

It is important for pregnant women to eat healthy.

low birth weight, two conditions associated with many serious developmental problems. Pregnancy increases a woman's dietary need for calories (energy), proteins, fluids, and certain vitamins and minerals such as folacin, Vitamins C and D, iron, and calcium. While vitamin supplements may be prescribed, they are not a substitute for a nutritious diet. The body must have essential nutrients and fibers before it can utilize vitamins in tablet form.

Weight
What is the optimum weight gain during pregnancy? This question has been debated for decades. Today, most doctors agree that a woman should gain approximately 22 to 25 pounds over the nine month period. Gains considerably under or over this range can increase risks for both mother and child during pregnancy and at the time of birth. Following a diet that is nutritionally adequate helps to ensure optimum weight gain. Consuming too many empty calories such as those found in junk foods, sweets, and alcohol, often leads to excessive weight gain. It also deprives both mother and fetus of critical nutrients found in a well-balanced diet.

Rest and Stress
Pregnancy often increases fatigue and strain on the mother's body. Additional sleep and occasional periods of rest may help ease these problems. Pregnancy

also may induce or increase emotional stress. Prolonged or excessive stress can have negative effects on the fetus by reducing breathing rate, heart beat, and activity level. While it may not be possible for a pregnant woman to avoid all stress, strain, and fatigue, the ill effects can be lessened with proper rest, nutrition, and exercise.

Age and General Health

A woman's age at the time of conception is an important factor in fetal development. Numerous studies conclude that the early to late twenties are the optimum years for childbearing. The rate of death and developmental disability among babies born to teenage mothers is nearly double that of babies born to women in their twenties. The immaturity of a teenager's reproductive system increases the risk of giving birth to premature or low birth weight babies. Also, teen mothers often lack access to prenatal care, adequate nourishment and housing, and have limited education, especially about caring for a child.

Pregnancy in older women (late thirties and beyond) presents other concerns. The chances of having a child with certain birth defects—Down syndrome, for example—are greater with maternal aging because genetic material in the ova deteriorates as women grow older, thus increasing the probability of such disorders. Older women also tend to experience a higher incidence of medical problems during pregnancy. On the other hand, mothers who are physically fit and have good medical care have a good chance of giving birth to healthy babies.

Increasingly sophisticated technology is contributing to reductions in fetal risk for mothers of all ages. The availability of more knowledgeable genetic counseling, as well as ultrasound scanning (sonogram), **CVS**, and amniocentesis, allow medical personnel to monitor fetal growth and identify particular problems. These procedures are especially useful for many of today's women who are electing to delay childbearing until their late thirties and early forties.

While the risks of pregnancy are undeniably greater for older women and teenagers, the problems often have as much to do with poverty as with age. (Exceptions are the chromosomal abnormalities such as Down syndrome). Vast numbers of fetal problems, regardless of maternal age, are closely associated with lack of medical care, poor nutrition, substandard housing, and limited education, all closely associated with poverty.

CVS—Chronic villus sampling in which a needle is inserted and cells are taken from what will be the placenta.

THREATS TO OPTIMUM FETAL DEVELOPMENT

Much is known about how to have a healthy baby; much is known, too, about the substances and maternal practices that lower those odds. Factors that have negative effects on the developing fetus are known as **teratogens**. Some are especially damaging during the earliest weeks of pregnancy, a particularly sensitive period when the baby's major organs and body systems are being formed. Teratogens that have been identified through extensive research include:

- consumption of alcohol;
- maternal smoking;
- addictive drugs, such as cocaine, heroin, amphetamines;
- hazardous chemicals; for example, mercury, lead, carbon monoxide, PCBs;
- radiation;
- some medications, among them, tranquilizers, hormones, antihistamines;
- maternal infections, such as rubella (German measles), syphillis, herpes, cytomegalovirus, AIDS, toxoplasmosis.

Researchers are also examining several controversial issues to determine a possible link with birth defects. These include:

- prolonged exposure to high temperatures (hot baths, saunas, hot tubs);
- pesticides;
- secondary smoke;
- certain over–the–counter medications;
- electromagnetic fields, such as those created by heating pads, electric blankets, and proximity to high voltage lines.

Because many substances can, and do, cross the placental barrier, women who are even contemplating pregnancy should avoid unnecessary contacts with known teratogens. As noted earlier, fetal organs and body systems are especially vulnerable to such agents during the first weeks following conception. This is not to imply that there is ever a completely "safe" period. Even in the later months, fetal growth can be seriously affected by maternal exposure to, or use of, substances mentioned here and in the following sections.

Alcohol

A mother's alcohol consumption during pregnancy can have serious consequences for the developing fetus. It can result in what now is diagnosed as Fetal Alcohol Syndrome (FAS) or Fetal Alcohol Effect (FAE). These children with FAS display a variety of abnormalities, including stunted growth, smaller brain size, facial irregularities, heart defects, and behavior and learning problems. Fetal death from maternal alcohol use also occurs. How much alcohol it takes to damage the fetus has not been determined; as little as an ounce or less per day (an amount once considered "safe") may be damaging. Alcohol should be used cautiously during the childbearing years and avoided completely during pregnancy.

Smoking

Serious fetal malformations and birth complications have been linked to maternal smoking. Cigarette smoke contains substances, such as nicotine and carbon monoxide, that cross the placental barrier and interfere with normal fetal development. Carbon monoxide, for example, reduces the amount of oxygen available to the fetus; this early oxygen deprivation seems to correlate with learning and behavior problems, especially as exposed children reach school age. Also, babies of mothers who smoke tend to be of below-average birth weight; they are also more likely to be premature, stillborn, or die shortly after birth.

Chemicals and Drugs

Numerous chemicals and drugs are known to have an adverse effect on the developing fetus; these substances range from prescription medications to "street" drugs. Some cause severe malformations, such as missing or malformed limbs or facial features. Others lead to fetal death (spontaneous abortion), premature birth, or behavior and learning disabilities during childhood and youth. Not all exposed fetuses will be affected in the same manner or to the same degree. The nature and severity of an infant's abnormalities seem to be influenced by the timing of exposure during fetal development and the amount and type of substance that the mother used. Research does not yet provide a definitive answer as to which drugs and chemicals (if any) have absolutely no harmful effects on the developing fetus; therefore, women who are or may become pregnant should be extremely cautious about using any chemical substance or medication except under medical supervision. They should also avoid exposure to previously discussed environmental hazards, particularly in the early stages of pregnancy.

Maternal Infections

While the placenta effectively filters out many infectious organisms, it cannot prevent all disease–causing agents from reaching the unborn child. Some of these agents are known to cause fetal abnormalities. The type of abnormality depends on the mother's illness and stage of pregnancy when infection occurs. For example, a pregnant woman who develops rubella (German measles) during the first four to eight weeks following conception is at high risk for giving birth to an infant who has heart problems, or is deaf, blind, or both (a tragic example of the extreme vulnerability of the fetus during its earliest weeks).

NOTE: Rubella can be controlled if women who do not have natural immunity receive vaccinations after or not less than 3 to 4 months prior to pregnancy.

Fortunately, only a small percentage of babies exposed to infectious agents will experience abnormalities. It is still unknown why only some babies are affected. What is reasonably certain is that pregnant women who are well-nourished, have good prenatal care, and are generally healthy and free of addictive substances and other excesses have a high probability of giving birth to a strong and healthy baby.

REVIEW QUESTIONS

1. Identify three practices that improve a mother's chances of having a healthy baby:
   a.

   b.

   c.

2. List three factors that appear to be hazardous to fetal development:
   a.

   b.

   c.

3. Identify one characteristic of fetal development that occurs during each stage:
   a.

   b.

   c.

TRUE/FALSE

1. A father's health status has no effect on the unborn child.

2. The younger a mother, the healthier her baby will be.

3. The embryonic stage is the most critical in terms of fetal development.

4. A zygote results when an egg and sperm unite.

5. Pregnancy increases a mother's need for calcium, iron, folacin, and Vitamins A and D.

6. The placenta is effective in protecting a fetus from all harmful substances.

7. Maternal smoking can cause lowered birth weight.

8. Pregnant women should avoid exercise because it can cause a miscarriage.

MULTIPLE CHOICE. Select one or more correct answers from the lists below.

1. Women over age thirty-five
   a. often have more difficulty getting pregnant.
   b. make better mothers because they are more mature.
   c. run a greater risk of having a child with a developmental defect.

2. Teratogens are
   a. more harmful to the fetus in the early weeks of pregnancy.
   b. substances that interfere with normal fetal development. ⌣
   c. the products of early cell division.

3. During pregnancy, poverty typically increases the risks to mother and fetus because
   a. prenatal care often is not available.
   b. a nutritionally–adequate diet may be lacking.
   c. substance abuse is more common.

4. Fetal abnormalities can be detected early in the pregnancy by
   a. amniocentesis.
   b. x-ray.
   c. sonograms.

5. Mothers who smoke during pregnancy are more likely to give birth to babies who
   a. have respiratory problems.
   b. are born prematurely and have below-average birth weight.
   c. experience a higher incidence of allergies.

CHAPTER 4

The Infant

NEWBORN BIRTH TO 28 DAYS

The newborn infant is truly amazing. Within moments of birth it begins to adapt to an outside world that is radically different from the one experienced in utero. All body systems are in place and ready to function at the time of birth. The newborn's body immediately assumes responsibility for breathing, eating, eliminating, and regulating its body temperature; however, these systems are still immature, making the newborn completely dependent on parents and caregivers for survival.

Motor development (movement) is both reflexive and protective. There is no voluntary control of the body during the early weeks. Although newborn babies sleep most of the time, they are not passive. They are sensitive to their environment and have unique methods of responding to it. Crying is their primary method of communicating, of expressing needs and emotions. Perceptual and cognitive abilities are present, but they are impossible to distinguish from one another at this stage.

DEVELOPMENTAL PROFILES AND GROWTH PATTERNS

Growth and Physical Characteristics
The newborn's physical characteristics during the first few days of life are different from those of a slightly older infant. The skin is wrinkled. Within the first few days it will dry out and possibly peel in some areas. Skin color of all babies is relatively light, but will gradually darken to a shade characteristic of their racial background. The head may appear to have an unusual shape as a result of the birth process, but it will assume a normal shape within the first week. Hair color and amount varies with the individual baby.

- Average weight at birth is 6.5 to 9 pounds (3.0–4.1 kg); females weigh approximately 7 pounds (3.2 kg), males 7.5 pounds (3.4 kg).
- Five to seven percent of birth weight is lost in the days immediately following birth.

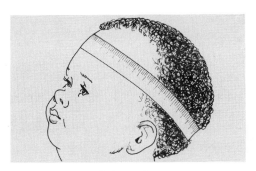

Head circumference

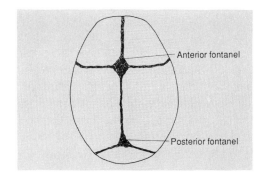

Fontanels

- An average of 5–6 ounces (.14–.17 kg) is gained per week during the first month.
- Average length at birth ranges from 18 to 21 inches (45.7–53.3 cm).
- Respiration (breathing) rate is approximately 30 to 50 breaths per minute.
- Chest appears small and cylindrical; it is nearly the same size as the head.
- Normal body temperature ranges from 96F. to 99F. (35.6–37.2 C).
- Regulation of body temperature is difficult during the first few weeks due to immature body systems and the thin layer of fat beneath the skin.
- Heart rate (pulse) ranges from 120 to 150 beats per minute; may be irregular at times.
- Skin is sensitive, especially on the hands and mouth.
- Head is large in relation to body; accounts for nearly one-fourth of the total body length.
- Head circumference averages 12.5 to 14.5 inches (31.7–36.8 cm) at birth.
- "Soft" spots (**fontanels**) are located on the top (anterior) and back (posterior) of the head.
- Breathing is often irregular in rhythm and rate.
- Tongue appears large in proportion to mouth.
- Crying is without tears.
- Eyes are extremely sensitive to light.
- Sees outlines and shapes; unable to focus on distant objects.

Motor Development
The newborn's motor skills are purely reflexive movements and are primarily for protection and survival. During the first month, the infant begins to gain some control over several of these early reflexes.

---

fontanels—Small openings in the infant's skull bones, covered with a soft tissue. Eventually they grow closed (sometimes called "soft spots").

- Engages in motor activity that is primarily reflexive:
  —Swallowing, sucking, gagging, coughing, yawning, blinking and elimination reflexes are present at birth.
  —Rooting reflex is triggered by gently touching sensitive skin around the cheek and mouth; the infant turns toward the cheek being stroked.
  —Startle reflex is set off by sudden, loud noises; both arms are thrown open and away from the body, then quickly return.
  —Moro reflex is brought about by quickly lowering the infant's position downward (as if dropping); arms are thrown open and quickly brought back together over the chest.
  —Grasping reflex occurs when the infant tightly curls its fingers around an object placed in its hand.
  —Stepping reflex involves the infant moving the feet up and down in walking-like movements when held upright with feet touching a firm surface.
  —Tonic neck reflex (TNR) occurs when the infant, in supine (face up) position, extends arm and leg on the side toward which the head is turned; the opposite arm and leg are flexed (pulled in toward the body); this is sometimes called the "fencing position."
  —Plantar reflex is the curling of toes when pressure is placed against the ball of foot.
- Maintains "fetal" position (back flexed or rounded, extremities held close to the body, knees drawn up) especially when asleep.
- Holds hands in a fist; does not reach for objects.

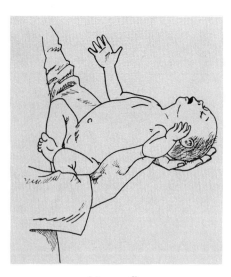

Moro reflex

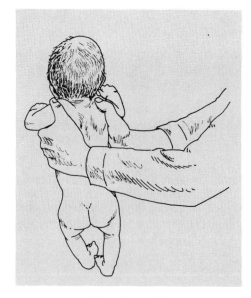

Stepping reflex

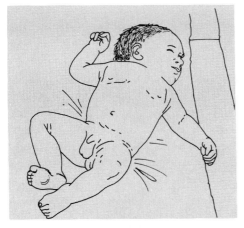

Tonic neck reflex

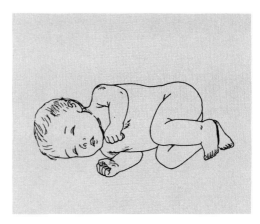

Sleeping in fetal position

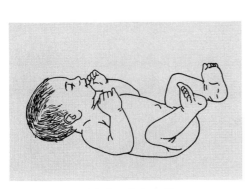

Holds hands in a fist

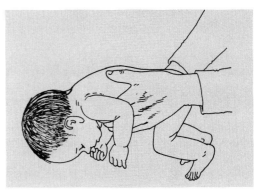

Prone suspension

- When held in a prone (face down) position, baby's head falls lower than the horizontal line of the body with hips flexed and arms and legs hanging down.
- Has good muscle tone in the upper body when supported under the arms.
- Turns head from side to side when placed in a prone (face down) position.
- **Pupils** dilate (enlarge) and constrict (become smaller).
- Eyes do not always work together and may appear crossed at times.
- Makes somewhat coordinated eye and head movements to track (follow) objects that are out of direct line of vision.

---

pupils—The small, dark, central portion of the eye.

Perceptual-Cognitive Development

The newborn's perceptual-cognitive skills are designed to capture and hold the attention of parents and caregivers and to gain some sense of the environment. Hearing is the most well-developed of the perceptual skills. Newborns can hear and respond to differences among certain sounds and are especially responsive to mother's voice. Sounds and movements such as crooning, rocking and jiggling seem to be soothing. Newborns also respond to being touched over most of the body, with mouth and hands being the most sensitive. Vision is present although limited. The newborn can focus both eyes, see objects up close, and follow slowly moving objects. From the earliest days of life, newborns absorb information through all of their senses, learning from what they see, hear, touch, taste, and smell. Purely reflexive behaviors are the major characteristic of the newborn's cognitive efforts. These take the form of sucking, startle responses, grimacing, flailing of arms and legs, and eye movements. As noted earlier, these responses overlap with perceptual responses.

- Gives a partial irregular eye blink to a fast-approaching object.
- Follows a slowly moving object through a complete arc of 180 degrees.
- Follows objects moved vertically if object is close to infant's face (10–15 inches; 25.4–38.1 cm).
- Continues looking about even in the dark.
- Begins to study own hand when lying in tonic neck reflex (TNR) position.
- Hearing is present at birth and is more acute than vision. Infants hear as well as adults, except for quiet sounds.

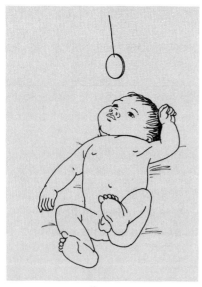

Follows vertically moving objects

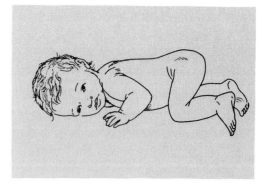

Studies own hand

- Prefers to listen to mother's voice rather than a stranger's.
- Often synchronizes body movements to speech patterns of parent or caregiver.
- Distinguishes some tastes; shows preference for sweet liquids.
- Sense of smell present at birth; will turn away from strong, unpleasant odors.

Speech and Language

The beginnings of speech and language development can be identified in several of the newborn's reflexes. These include the bite-release action that occurs when the infant's gums are rubbed, the rooting reflex, and the sucking reflex. In addition, the new baby communicates directly and indirectly in a number of other ways.

- Crying and fussing are major forms of communication.
- Reacts to loud noises by blinking, moving, stopping a movement, shifting eyes about, or making a startle response.
- Shows a preference for certain sounds, such as music and human voices, by calming down or quieting.
- Turns head in response to voice on either side.
- Makes occasional sounds other than crying.

Personal-Social Development

Newborns are skilled at interacting socially. They indicate needs and distress and respond to parent's or caregiver's reactions to these behaviors. The infant thrives on feelings of security and soon displays a sense of attachment to primary caregivers.

- Experiences a short period of alertness immediately following birth.
- Sleeps 17 to 19 hours per day; gradually is awake and responsive for longer times.
- Likes to be held close and cuddled when awake.
- Shows qualities of individuality; each infant varies in ways of responding or not responding to similar situations.
- Begins to establish emotional attachment or **"bonding"** relationship with parents and caregivers.
- Begins to develop a sense of security or feeling of trust with parents and caregivers; responses to different individuals vary. For example, the infant may become tense with a caregiver who is uncomfortable with infant.

---

bonding—The establishment of a close, loving relationship between an infant and adult, usually the mother and father, is called bonding; sometimes called attachment.

DAILY ROUTINES—BIRTH TO 28 DAYS

Eating

- Takes 6 to 10 feedings, a total of approximately 22 oz. or 660 ml per 24 hours at the beginning of this period; later the number will be reduced to 5 or 6.
- Drinks 2 to 4 ounces of breast milk or formula per feeding.
- Takes from 25 to 30 minutes to complete a feeding.
- Expresses the need for food by crying.

Bathing, Dressing, Toileting Needs.

- Signals the need for diaper change by crying (if crying does not stop when diaper has been changed another cause should be sought).
- Enjoys bath; keeps eyes open and gives other indications of pleasure when placed in warm water.
- Expresses displeasure when clothes are pulled over head (best to avoid over-the-head-clothes).
- Enjoys being wrapped firmly (swaddled) in a blanket; swaddling seems to foster feelings of security and comfort.
- Has 1 to 4 bowel movements per day.

Sleeping

- After the first few days, has 4 to 6 sleep periods per 24 hours; one of these may be 5 to 7 hours in length.
- Falls asleep toward the end of feeding.
- Cries before falling asleep (usually stops if held and rocked briefly).

Play and Social Activities

- Enjoys light and brightness; may fuss if turned away from the light.
- Stares at faces in close visual range (10–12 inches; 25.4–30.5 cm).
- Signals the need for social stimulation by crying; stops when picked up or put in infant seat close to voices and movement.
- Content to lie on back much of the time.
- Before being picked up, need to be forewarned by first being touched and talked to.
- Enjoys lots of touching, fondling, and holding; may become fussy with over-stimulation.
- Enjoys "en face" (face to face) position.

LEARNING ACTIVITIES

The first month.

Tips for parents and caregiver.

- Respond with gentle and dependable adult attention to baby's cries so baby learns that help is always available; (infants always cry for a reason; crying signals a need).
- Make eye-to-eye contact when baby is in an alert state; make faces or stick out your tongue, activities which new babies often imitate (imitation is an important avenue for learning).
- Talk or sing to baby in a normal voice during feeding, diapering, bathing; vary voice tone and rhythm of speech.
- Recognize and show delight in baby's responsiveness. (Mutual responsiveness and social turn-taking is the basis for all teaching and learning in the months and years ahead.)
- Show pictures of simple design (new babies tend to prefer simple drawings of faces); gently move a stuffed animal or toy 10 to 15 inches from baby's face to encourage visual tracking; hang toys or mobile within baby's visual range (change often).
- Take cues from baby; too much stimulation can be as distressing as too little.

DEVELOPMENTAL ALERTS

Check with a health care provider or early childhood specialist if, by one month of age, the infant *does not*:

- Show alarm or "startle" responses to loud noise
- Suck and swallow with ease.
- Show gains in height, weight, and head circumference.
- Grasp with equal strength in both hands.
- Make eye-to-eye contact when awake and being held.
- Becomes quiet soon after being picked up.
- Roll head from side to side when placed on stomach.

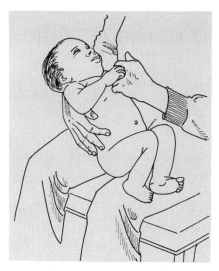

Stops crying when held

- Expresses needs and emotions with unique cries and patterns of vocalizations that can be distinguished from one another.
- Stops crying when picked up and held.

ONE TO FOUR MONTHS

During these early months, more of the wonders of infancy begin to unfold. The infant continues to grow at a fast rate. Body systems are fairly well stabilized with body temperature, breathing patterns, and heart rate becoming more regular. Longer periods of wakefulness contribute to the infant's personal-social development. Social responsiveness increases as infants practice and enjoy using their eyes to explore the environment. Infants also begin to find great pleasure in imitating the speech sounds and gestures of others. Increased social awareness allows the infant to begin to establish a sense of trust and emotional attachment to parents and caregivers.

Crying remains the primary way of communicating and of gaining adult attention. However, infants' communication skills soon expand to include body gestures and many non-crying behaviors. Increased strength and voluntary control of muscles contribute to improved motor development. These newly acquired skills are put to constant use throughout the infants' waking hours. During these early months, it must be noted once again that perceptual, cognitive and motor development are closely interrelated and nearly impossible to differentiate. Learning takes place continuously as the infant explores and acquires information about a still new and strange environment.

DEVELOPMENTAL PROFILES AND GROWTH PATTERNS

Growth and Physical Characteristics

- Average length is 20 to 27 inches (50.8–68.6 cm); grows approximately 1 inch (2.54 cm) per month (measured with infant lying on back, from top of the head to bottom of heel, knees straight and foot flexed).
- Weighs an average of 8 to 16 pounds (3.6–7.3 kg); females weighing slightly less than males.
- Gains approximately $1/4$ to $1/2$ lb. per week (.11–.22 kg).
- Respiration rate is approximately 30 to 40 breaths per minute; increases significantly during periods of crying or activity.
- Normal body temperature ranges from 96.4 to 99.6 F (35.7–37.5 C).
- Head and chest circumference are nearly equal.
- Head circumference increases approximately $3/4$ inch (1.9 cm) per month until 2 months, then increases $5/8$ inch (1.6 cm) per month until 4 months. Increases are important indication of continued brain growth.
- Heart rate (pulse) is approximately 120 to 150 beats per minute at rest.
- Continues to breathe using abdominal (stomach) muscles.
- Posterior fontanel ("soft spot" at back of head) closes by the second month.
- Anterior fontanel ("soft spot" on top of head) closes to approximately $1/2$ inch (1.3 cm).
- Skin remains sensitive and easily irritated.
- Arms and legs are of equal length, size, and shape; easily flexed and extended.
- Legs may appear slightly bowed.
- Feet appear flat with no arch.
- Cries with tears.
- Eyes begin moving together in unison (binocular vision).
- Color vision is present.

Motor Development

- Reflexive motor behaviors are changing:
  —Tonic neck and stepping reflexes disappear.
  —Rooting and sucking reflexes are well-developed.
  —Swallowing reflex and tongue movements are still immature; continued drooling and inability to move food to the back of the mouth.
  —Landau reflex appears near the middle of this period; when baby is held in a prone (face down) position the head is held upright and legs are fully extended.
- Grasps objects with entire hand; strength insufficient to hold items.

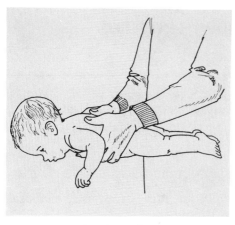

Landau reflex

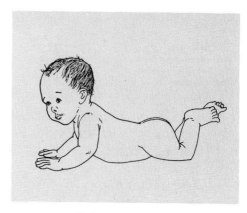

Raises up on arms

- Holds hands in an open or semi-open position.
- Muscle tone and development is equal for boys and girls.
- Muscle strength and control improving; early movements are large and jerky; gradually become smoother and move purposeful.
- Raises head and upper body on arms when in a prone position.
- Turns head to side when in a supine (face up) position; near the end of this period head is held erect and in line with the body.
- Upper body parts are more active: clasps hands above face, waves arms about, reaches for objects.

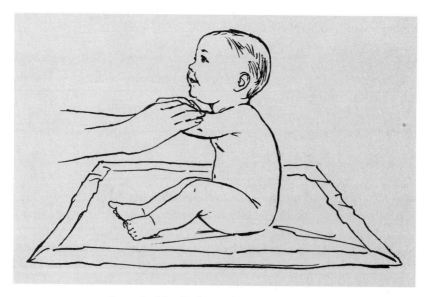

An arched back shows the lumbar curve.

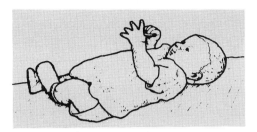

Actively plays with hands

- At first, infant rolls from front to back by turning head to one side and allowing trunk to follow; later, infant rolls onto its side. Near the end of this period, infant can roll from front to back to side at will.
- Can be pulled to a sitting position, with considerable head lag and rounded back at the beginning of this period. Later, can be positioned to sit, with minimal head support. Near the end of this period, the infant sits with support, holds head steady, and keeps back fairly erect; enjoys sitting in an infant seat or being held on a lap.

Perceptual-Cognitive Development

- Fixates on a moving object held at 12 inches (30.5 cm); smoother visual tracking of objects across 180 degree pathway, vertically and horizontally.

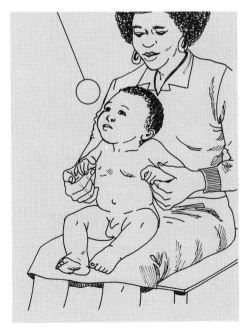

Follows a moving object vertically and horizontally

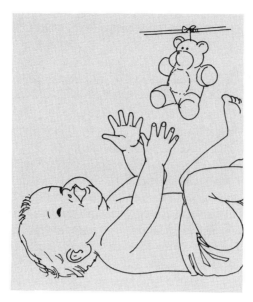

Focuses and reaches for objects

- Continues to gaze in direction of moving objects that disappear.
- Exhibits some sense of size, color, and shape recognition of objects in the immediate environment—for example, recognizes own bottle even when bottle is turned about, thus presenting a different shape.
- Does not search for a bottle that falls out of a crib or for a toy hidden under a blanket: "Out of sight, out of mind."
- Watches hands intently.
- Moves eyes from one object to another.
- Focuses on small object and reaches for it; follows hands' movements with eyes.
- Alternates looking at an object, at one or both hands, and then back to the object.
- Imitates gestures that are modelled; bye–bye, patting head.
- Hits at object closest to right or left hand with some degree of accuracy.
- Localizes the source of a sound.
- Connects sound and rhythms with movement by moving or jiggling in time to music, singing, or chanting.
- Can distinguish parent's face from stranger's face when other cues such as voice, touch or smell are also available. (Not clear that this age infant can tell the difference between parent and stranger or even mother or father).
- Attempts to keep toy in motion by repeating arm or leg movements that started the toy moving in the first place.
- Begins to mouth objects.

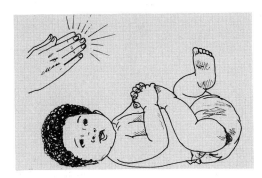

Turns toward sound

Speech and Language Development

- Reacts (stops whimpering, startles, turns head) to sounds such as a voice, rattle of a spoon, ringing of a bell.
- Coordinates vocalizing, looking, and body movements in face–to–face exchanges with parent or caregiver; can follow and lead in keeping communication going.
- Babbles or coos when spoken to or smiled at.
- Produces single vowel sounds (ah, eh, uh); also imitates own sounds and vowel sounds produced by others.

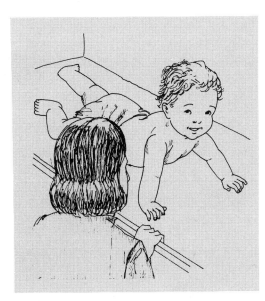

Responds with a social smile

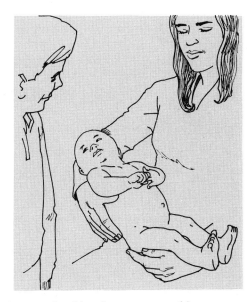

Looking for person speaking

- Searches for source of voice (turns head, eyes look for speaker).
- Laughs out loud.

Personal-Social Development

- Uses eyes to imitate, maintain, terminate, and avoid interactions—for example, infant turns at will, toward or away from a person or situation.
- Reacts differently to adult voices, may frown or look anxious if voices are loud, angry, or unfamiliar.
- Enjoys being held and cuddles at times other than feeding and bedtime.
- Coos, gurgles, and squeals when awake.
- Smiles in response to a friendly face or voice.
- Can entertain self by playing with fingers, hands, and toes.
- Enjoys familiar routines, such as being bathed and having diaper changed.
- Delights in play that involves gentle tickling, laughing, and jiggling.
- Spends much less time crying.
- Recognizes and reaches out to familiar faces and objects, such as the father or bottle; reacts by waving arms and squealing with excitement.
- Stops crying when parent or caregiver comes near.

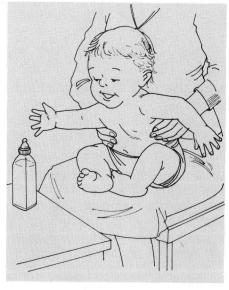

Recognizes and enjoys familiar routines

DAILY ROUTINES—1 TO 4 MONTHS

Eating

- Takes 5 to 8 feedings, each 5 to 6 ounces, per day.
- Begins fussing before anticipated feeding times; does not always cry to signal the need to eat.
- Needs only a little assistance in getting nipple to mouth; beginning to help by using own hands to guide nipple.
- Sucks vigorously; may choke on occasion with the vigor and enthusiasm of sucking.
- Becomes impatient if bottle or breast continues to be offered once hunger is satisfied.
- Not ready to eat solid foods.

Bathing, Dressing, Toilet Needs

- May enjoy bath; kicks, laughs and splashes.
- Has one or two bowel movements per day; frequently skips a day.
- Establishing a regular time for bowel movements according to infant's own pattern.

Sleep

- Often falls asleep for the night soon after the evening feeding.
- Begins to sleep through the night; many babies do not sleep more than 6 hours at a stretch for several more months.
- Averages $14^1/_2$ to 17 hours of sleep per day; often awake for 2 or 3 periods during the daytime.
- Thumbsucking may begin during this period.
- Entertains self before falling asleep: "talks", plays with hands, jiggles crib.

Play and Social Activity

- Spends waking periods in physical activity; kicking, turning head from side to side, clasping hands together, grasping objects.
- Becoming "talkative"; vocalizes with delight.
- Likes being talked to and sung to; may cry when the social interaction ends.
- Appears happy when awake and alone (for short periods of time).

LEARNING ACTIVITIES

One to four months.

Tips for parents and caregivers.

- Imitate baby's vocalizations and faces (grunting, smacking, yawning, squinting, frowning). When baby begins to smile, smile back and sometimes remark: "You are smiling! Nice smile."
- Read to baby, out of magazines, books, whatever interests you; it's the sound of your voice and your closeness that matters.
- Play simplified peek-a-boo (hold cloth in front of your own face, drop it, say *peek-a-boo*); repeat if baby shows interest.
- Gently stretch and bend baby's arms and legs while making up an accompanying song; later, start a gentle "bicycling" activity.
- Touch baby's hand with a small toy* (soft rattles or other noisemakers are especially good); encourage baby to grasp toy.
- Walk around with baby, touching and naming objects. Stand with baby in front of mirror, touching and naming facial features: "Baby's mouth, mommy's mouth. Baby's eye, mommy's eye."
- Attach an unbreakable mirror to crib, or to a wall close to the crib, so baby can look and talk to him or herself.
- Fasten (*securely*) small bells to baby's bootees; this helps baby to localize sounds and learn, at the same time, that he or she has power, can make things happen simply by moving about.

* Toys and other objects given to an infant should be no smaller than the baby's fist in order to prevent choking or swallowing.

DEVELOPMENTAL ALERTS

Check with a health care provider or early childhood specialist if, by four months of age, the infant *does not*:

- Continue to show steady and measurable increases in height, weight, and head circumference.
- Smile in response to the smiles of others (the social smile is a significant developmental milestone).
- Follow a moving object with eyes focusing together.
- Bring hands together over mid-chest.
- Turn head to locate sounds.
- Begin to raise head and upper body when placed on stomach.
- Reach for objects or familiar persons.

FOUR TO EIGHT MONTHS

Between four and eight months the infant is developing a wide range of skills and great variability in using his or her body. Infants seem to be busy every waking moment. They manipulate and mouth toys and other objects that come to hand. They "talk" all the time, making vowel and consonant sounds in ever greater variety and complexity. They initiate social interactions and respond to all kinds of cues, such as facial expressions, gestures, and the comings and goings of everyone in the infant's world. Infants at this age are both self-contained and sociable. They move easily from spontaneous, self-initiated activity to social activities initiated by others.

DEVELOPMENTAL PROFILES AND GROWTH PATTERNS

Growth and Physical Characteristics

- Gains approximately 1 lb. (2.2 kg) per month in weight.
- Doubles original birth weight.
- Gains approximately $1/2$ inch (1.3 cm) in length per month; average length is 27.5 to 29 inches (69.8–73.7 cm).
- Head and chest circumferences are nearly equal.
- Head circumference increases approximately $3/8$ inch (0.95 cm) per month until 6 to 7 months, then $3/16$ inch (0.47 cm) per month; head circumference should continue to increase steadily, indicating healthy, on-going brain growth.
- Pulse (heart rate) remains approximately 100 to 140 beats per minute; rate is affected by infant's activity level.
- Breathing is abdominal; ranges from 25 to 50 breaths per minute depending on amount of stimulation; rate and patterns vary from infant to infant.
- Teeth begin to appear with upper and lower incisors coming in first, gums may be red and swollen. There may also be increased drooling, chewing, biting, and mouthing of objects.
- Legs may appear bowed; bowing gradually disappears as infant grows older.
- True eye color is established.

Motor Development

- Reflexive behaviors are changing:
  —Blinking reflex is well-established
  —Sucking reflex becomes voluntary

Chews and mouths objects

—Moro reflex disappears
—Parachute reflex appears toward the end of this stage (when held in a prone, horizontal position and lowered suddenly, infant throws out arms as a protective measure).
—Swallowing reflex appears (a more complex form of swallowing that involves tongue movement against the roof of mouth); allows infant to move solid foods from front of mouth to the back for swallowing.
• Uses finger and thumb (pincer grip) to pick up objects.
• Reaches for objects with both arms simultaneously; later reaches with one hand or the other.

Sucking becomes voluntary

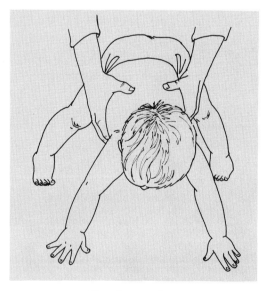

Parachute reflex

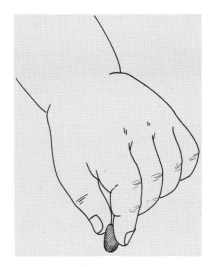

Transfers objects from one hand to the other   **Pincer grasp**

- Transfers objects from one hand to the other; grasps object using entire hand (palmar grasp).
- Handles, shakes, and pounds objects; puts everything into mouth.
- Holds own bottle.
- Sits alone without support, holding head erect, and arms propped forward for support.
- Pulls self into a crawling position by raising up on arms and drawing knees up beneath the body; rocks back and forth, but generally does not move forward.
- Lifts head when placed on back.
- Rolls over from front to back and back to front.

Palmar grasp

- May accidentally begin scooting backwards when placed on stomach; soon will begin to crawl forward.
- Enjoys being placed in standing position, especially on someone's lap; jumps in place.

Perceptual-Cognitive Development

- Turns toward and locates familiar voices and sounds: these cues can be used to informally test an infant's hearing.
- Focuses eyes on small objects and reaches for them.
- Uses hand, mouth, and eyes in coordination to explore own body, toys, and surroundings.
- Imitates actions such as pat-a-cake, waving bye-bye, and playing peek-a-boo.
- Shows fear of falling off high places such as changing table, stairs; depth perception is clearly evident.
- Looks over side of crib or high chair for objects dropped; delights in repeatedly throwing objects overboard for caregiver to retrieve.
- Searches for toy or food that has been completely hidden under cloth or behind screen; beginning to understand that objects continue to exist even whey they cannot be seen. (Piaget refers to this as "object permanence.")
- Handles and explores objects in a variety of ways; visually; turning them around; feeling all surfaces; banging and shaking them.
- Picks up inverted object (in other words, recognizes it's a cup even though it is positioned differently).
- Unable to deal with more than one toy at a time; may either ignore second toy or drop toy in one hand and focus vision on the new toy.
- Reaches accurately with either hand.
- Plays actively with small toys, such as rattle.

Plays pat-a-cake

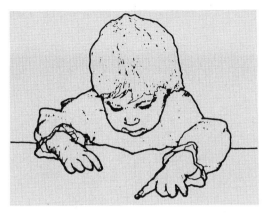

Inspects objects with eyes and hands

Recognizes inverted but familiar objects

- Bangs objects together playfully; bangs spoon on table.
- Holds small object in one hand while reaching toward another object.
- Continues to take everything to mouth.
- Full attachment to mother or single caregiver. Coincides with growing understanding of "object permanence", the idea that objects exist even when they are no longer visible.

Speech and Language Development

- Responds appropriately to familiar words, such as "daddy" and "go bye-bye?"

Holds one toy while reaching for another

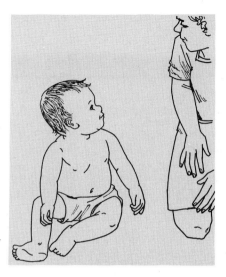

Responds to own name

- Responds to own name.
- Imitates some nonspeech sounds, such as cough, tongue click, lip smacking.
- Produces a full range of vowels and some consonants: *r, s, z, th*, and *w*.
- Responds to variations in the tone of voice of others—anger, playfulness, sadness.
- Expresses emotions, such as pleasure, satisfaction, and anger by making different sounds.
- "Talks" to toys.
- Babbles by repeating same syllable in a series: *ba, ba, ba*.
- Responds to simple requests: "Wave bye-bye." "Come."

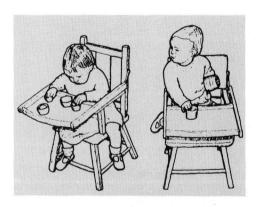

Turns to watch people and activities

- Makes different responses to vacuum cleaner, phone ringing, dog barking; may cry, whimper, or look toward parent or caregiver for reassurance.

Personal-Social Development

- Looks with interest at surroundings; continuously watching people and activities.
- Developing an awareness of self as a separate individual from others.
- More outgoing and social in nature: smiles, coos, reaches out.
- Can tell the difference between, and responds differently to, strangers, caretakers, parents, brothers and sisters.
- Responds differently and appropriately to facial expressions: frowns; smiles.
- Imitates facial expressions, actions, and sounds made by others.
- Still friendly toward strangers at the beginning of this stage; later is reluctant to be approached by, or left with, strangers; exhibits "stranger anxiety."
- Enjoys being held and cuddled; indicates desire to be picked up by raising arms.
- Establishes a trust relationship with parents and caregiver if physical and emotional needs are met consistently; by 6 months shows preference for major caregiver, often the mother.
- Laughs out loud.
- Becomes upset if toy or other objects are taken away.
- Seeks attention by using body movements, verbalizations, or both.

Still friendly with strangers

DAILY ROUTINES—4 TO 8 MONTHS

Eating

- Adjusts feeding times to the family's schedule; usually takes 3 or 4 feedings per day, each 6 to 8 ounces, depending upon sleep schedule.
- Shows interest in feeding activities; reaches for cup and spoon while being fed.
- Able to wait half hour or more after awakening for first morning feeding.
- Has less need for sucking.
- Begins to accept small amount of solid foods, such as banana and cereal, when placed well back on tongue (if placed on tip, infant will push it back out).
- Closes mouth firmly or turns head away when hunger is satisfied.

Toileting, Bathing, Dressing

- Enjoys being free of clothes.
- Splashes vigorously with both hands and sometimes feet during bathtime.
- Hands moving constantly; nothing within reach is safe from being spilled or dashed to floor.
- Pulls off own socks; plays with strings and buttons and velcro closures on clothing.
- Has one bowel movement per day as a general rule.
- Urinates often and in quantity; female infants tend to have longer intervals between wetting.

Sleeping

- Awakens between 6 and 8 a.m.; usually falls asleep soon after evening meal.
- No longer wakens for a late-night feeding.
- Sleeps 11 to 13 hours through the night.
- Takes 2 or 3 naps per day, (however, there is great variability among infants).

Play and Social Activity

- Enjoys lying on back; arches back, kicks, stretches legs upwards, grasps feet and brings them to mouth.
- Looks at own hands with interest and delight; may squeal or gaze at them intently.

- Enjoys playing with soft, squeaky toys and rattles; puts them in mouth, bites, and chews on them.
- "Talks" happily to self: gurgles, growls, makes high squealing sounds.
- Differentiates between people: lively with those who are familiar, anxious about or ignores others (this is sometimes referred to as a period of "stranger anxiety").
- Likes rhythmic activities: being bounced, jiggled, swung about gently.

LEARNING ACTIVITIES

Four to eight months.

Tips for parents and caregivers.

- Gradually elaborate on earlier activities: imitate baby's sounds, facial expressions, and body movements; name body parts; look in the mirror together and make faces; read and talk and sing to baby several times a day.
- Use baby's name during all kinds of activities so baby comes to recognize it: "*Kyle* is smiling", "*Carla's* eyes are wide open."
- Provide toys, rattles, and household items that make noise as baby shakes or waves them (a set of measuring spoons or plastic keys, shaker cans, squeak toys. Remember the "*Rule of fist.*")
- Fasten a cradle gym across the crib; a younger baby can swipe at objects and later actually connect (both activities are essential in learning eye-hand coordination. (Homemade cradle gyms made of safe household items are equally effective.)
- Play and move to radio or taped music with baby; vary the tempo and movement: gentle jiggling, dancing, turning in circles; dance in front of the mirror, describing movements to baby.
- Allow plenty of time for bathtime because it can provide important learnings in all areas of development and mutual enjoyment of learning activities.
- Play *This little piggy, Where's baby's* (nose, eye, hand…), and simple games invented on the spot such as taking turns at shaking rattles or gently bumping foreheads.

DEVELOPMENTAL ALERTS

Check with a health care provider or early childhood specialist if, by eight months of age, the infant *does not*:

- Show even, steady increase in weight, height, and head size, (too slow or too rapid growth are both cause for concern).
- Explore own hands and objects placed in hands.
- Hold and shake a rattle.
- Smile, babble, and laugh aloud.
- Search for hidden objects.
- Use finger and thumb (pincer grasp) to pick up objects.
- Have an interest in playing games, such as "pat-a-cake" and "peek-a-boo".
- Appear interested in new or unusual sounds.
- Reach for and grasp objects.
- Sit alone.
- Begin to eat some solid foods.

EIGHT TO TWELVE MONTHS

Between eight months and one year of age, the infant is gearing up for two major developmental events—walking and talking. These usually begin about the time of the first birthday. The infant is becoming skillful at manipulating small objects and spends a great deal of time practicing by picking up and releasing toys or whatever else is at hand. Infants at this age are also becoming extremely sociable. They find ways to be the center of attention and to get approval and applause from family and friends. When the applause is forthcoming, the infant joins in with unselfconscious delight. The ability to imitate is also developing. It will serve two purposes: to extend social interactions and to help the child learn many new skills and behaviors in the months of rapid development that lie ahead.

DEVELOPMENTAL PROFILES AND GROWTH PATTERNS

Growth and Physical Characteristics

- Gains in height are slower than during the previous months, averaging $1/2$ inch (1.3 cm) per month. Infants reach approximately $1 1/2$ times their birth length by their first birthday.

- Weight increases by approximately 1 pound (.5 kg) per month; birth weight nearly triples by 1 year of age: infants weigh an average of 21 pounds (9.6 kg).
- Heart rate averages 100 to 140 beats per minute, depending on activity.
- Respiration rates vary with activity; typically 20 to 45 breaths per minute.
- Body temperature ranges from 96.4 F. to 99.6 F. (35.7–37.5 C); still affected somewhat by environmental conditions: weather; activity; clothing.
- Head and chest circumference remain equal.
- Continues to use abdominal muscles for breathing.
- Anterior fontanel begins to close.
- Approximately 4 upper and 4 lower incisors and 2 lower molars erupt.
- Arm and hands are more developed than feet and legs (cephalo-caudal development); hands appear large in proportion to other body parts.
- Legs may continue to appear bowed.
- Feet appear flat as arch has not yet fully developed.
- Visual acuity is approximately 20/100.
- Both eyes working in unison (true binocular coordination).
- Can see distant objects (15–20 feet away) and points at them.

Motor Development

- Reaches with one hand leading in order to grasp an offered object or toy.
- Manipulates objects, transferring them from one hand to the other.
- Explores new objects by poking with one finger.
- Uses deliberate finger and thumb movement (pincer grasp) to pick up small objects, toys, and finger foods.

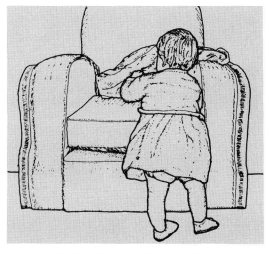

Pulls self to standing position

- Stacks objects; also places objects inside one another.
- Releases objects or toys by dropping or throwing; cannot intentionally put an object down.
- Beginning to pull self to a standing position.
- Beginning to stand alone, leaning on furniture for support; moves around objects by side-stepping.
- Has good balance when sitting; can shift positions without falling.
- Creeps on hands and knees; crawls up and down stairs.
- Walks with adult support, holding onto adult's hand; may begin to walk alone.

Perceptual-Cognitive Development

- Watches people, objects, and activities in the immediate environment.
- Shows awareness of distant objects (15 to 20 feet away) by pointing at them.
- Responds to hearing tests (voice localization); however loses interest quickly and, therefore, may be difficult to test informally.
- Follows simple instructions.
- Reaches for toys that are out of reach, but visible.
- Still takes everything to mouth.

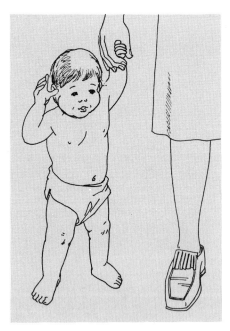

Walks with adult support

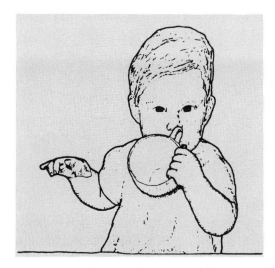

Puts everything in the mouth

- Continues to drop first item when trying to take three offered items.
- Recognizes the reversal of an object: cup upside down is still a cup.
- Imitates activities: hitting 2 blocks together, playing pat-a-cake.
- Drops toys intentionally and repeatedly; looks in direction of fallen object.
- Shows appropriate use of everyday items: pretends to drink from cup, put on necklace, hug doll, make stuffed animal "walk".
- Shows some sense of spacial relationships: puts block in cup and takes it out when requested to do so.
- Beginning to show an understanding of causality—for example, hands mechanical toy back to adult to have it rewound.
- Shows some awareness of the working relationship of objects: puts spoon in mouth; places cup on saucer; uses brush to smooth hair.
- Searches for partially hidden toy by the end of this period.

Speech and Language Development

- Babbles or jabbers deliberately to get a social interaction started; may shout to attract attention; listens, then shout again.
- Shakes head for no and may nod for yes.
- Responds by looking for voice when name is called.
- Babbling in sentence-like sequences; followed a bit later by jargon (syllables and sounds with language-like inflection).
- Waves "bye-bye"; claps hands when asked.
- Says "da-da" and "ma-ma."
- Imitates sounds that are similar to those the baby has already learned to make; will also imitate motor noises, tongue click, lip smacking, coughing.

- Enjoys rhymes and simple songs; vocalizes and dances to music.
- Hands toy or object to an adult when appropriate gestures accompany the request.

Personal-Social Development

- Exhibits a definite fear or reluctance toward strangers; clings to, or hides behind, parent or caregiver; resists separating from familiar adult ("stranger anxiety").
- Wants parent or caregiver to be in constant sight.
- Sociable and outgoing; enjoys being near, and included in, daily activities of family members and caregiver.
- Enjoys novel experiences and opportunities to examine new objects.
- Shows need to be picked up and held by extending arms upward, crying, or clinging to adult's legs.
- Begins to be assertive by resisting caregiver's requests; may kick, scream or throw self on the floor.
- Offers toys and objects to others.
- Often becomes attached to a favorite toy or blanket.
- Upon hearing own name, looks up and smiles at person who is speaking.
- Repeats behaviors that get attention; jabbers continuously.
- Carries out simple directions and requests; understands the meaning of "no."

Understands the use of everyday objects

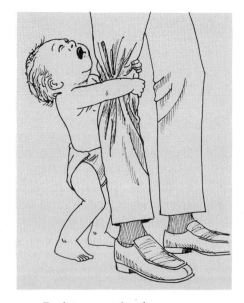

Resists separating from parent

DAILY ROUTINES—8 TO 12 MONTHS

Eating

- Eats three meals a day plus midmorning or midafternoon snacks, such as juice and crackers.
- Begins to refuse bottle (if this has not already occurred).
- Has good appetite.
- Enjoys drinking from a cup; holds own cup; will even tilt head backward to get the last bit.
- Begins to eat finger foods; may remove food from mouth, look at it, put it back in.
- Develops certain likes and dislikes for foods.
- Very active; infant's hands may be so busy that a toy is needed for each hand in order to prevent cup or dish from being turned over or food grabbed and tossed about.

Toileting, Bathing, Dressing

- Enjoys bath time; plays with washcloth, soap and water toys.
- Loves to let water drip from sponge or washcloth.
- Shows great interest in pulling off hats, taking shoes and socks off.
- Fusses when diaper needs changing; may pull off soiled or wet diaper.
- Cooperates to some degree in being dressed; helps put arm in arm holes, may even extend leg to have pants put on.
- Has one or two bowel movements per day.
- Occasionally dry after a nap.

Sleeping

- Willing to go to bed; may not go to sleep immediately, but will play or walk about in crib, then fall asleep on top of covers.
- Sleeps until 6 or 8 o'clock in the morning.
- Plays alone and quietly for 15 to 30 minutes after awakening; then begins to make demanding noises signaling the need to be up and about.
- Plays actively in crib when awake; crib sides must be up and securely fastened.
- Takes one afternoon nap most days.

Play and Social Activities

- Enjoys large motor activities: pulling to stand, cruising, standing alone, creeping. Some babies are walking at this point.
- Enjoys putting things on head: basket, bowl, cup; finds this very funny and expects people to notice and laugh.
- Puts objects in and out of each other: pans that nest, pegs in and out of a box.
- Enjoys hiding behind chairs to play "Where's baby?"
- Throws things on floor and expects them to be returned.
- Shows interest in opening and closing doors and cupboards.
- Gives an object to adult on request; expect to have it returned immediately.
- Responds to "no-no" by stopping; on the other hand, the infant may smile, laugh, and continue inappropriate behavior, thus making a game out of it.

LEARNING ACTIVITIES

Eight to Twelve Months.

Tips for parents and caregivers.

- Elaborate upon activities suggested earlier; always pick up on baby's lead whenever baby initiates a new response or *invents* a new version of a familiar game (the roots of creativity).
- Provide safe floor space close to parent or caregiver; learning to sit, crawl, stand, and explore are a baby's major occupations during these months.
- Read and tell tiny *stories* about everyday happenings in baby's life; also read from rugged, brightly colored picture books, allowing baby to help turn the pages.
- Talk about ongoing activities, emphasizing key words: "Here is the *soap*", "You are *squeezing* the sponge."
- Give baby simple instructions: "Pat mommy's head", "Pat baby's head." Allow adequate time to respond; if baby seems interested but does not respond, demonstrate the response.

- Accept baby's newly invented game of dropping things off of highchair tray or out of the crib; it's baby's way of learning about many things: cause and effect, gravity, adults' patience.
- Provide containers that baby can fill with small toys or other objects and them empty out. ("Rule of fist" still applies.)
- Give baby push and pull toys, roly-polys, toys with wheels. (Helping to unpack canned goods and rolling them across the kitchen floor is an all-time favorite game.)

DEVELOPMENTAL ALERTS

Check with a health care provider or early childhood specialist if, by 12 months of age, the infant *does not*:

- Blink when fast-moving objects approach the eye.
- Begin to cut teeth.
- Imitate simple sounds.
- Follow simple verbal requests: *come, bye bye*.
- Pull to stand.
- Transfer objects from hand to hand.
- Show anxiety toward strangers.
- Interact playfully with parents, caregivers, brothers and sisters.
- Feed self; hold own bottle or cup; pick up and eat finger foods.
- Creep or crawl.

REVIEW QUESTIONS

1. List three physical characteristics of the newborn infant.
   a.

   b.

   c.

2. List three ways in which it is possible to informally evaluate hearing in an infant who is not yet talking.

   a.

   b

   c.

3. List three reflexes present in the newborn that should disappear by the time the infant is a year old.

   a.

   b.

   c.

4. List three perceptual-cognitive skills that appear during the first year of life.

   a.

   b.

   c.

TRUE OR FALSE

1. Newborn infants are incapable of learning until they can stay awake for more than an hour or two at a time.

2. The newborn will alert (startle) in response to a loud noise.

3. Crying serves no useful developmental function except to let the infant signal hunger or a need to be changed or covered more warmly.

4. An infant's head circumference is measured regularly in order to assess brain growth.

5. Imitation should be discouraged in infants to ensure that they will not grow up to be "copy cats."

6. The healthy infant has nearly tripled its birth weight by one year of age.

7. All normally developing infants crawl in all fours before they walk.

8. The six-month-old who keeps throwing toys out of the crib should be scolded for causing extra work for the parent or caregiver.

9. Developmentally, there is no excuse for nine- or ten-month-old children to be afraid of strangers unless they have previously had a bad experience.

MULTIPLE CHOICE. Select one item in each of the following groupings that is *not* seen in the majority of infants in the age category listed.

1. Birth to 28 days
    a. cries without tears.
    b. synchronizes body movements to speech patterns of parent or caregiver.
    c. shows need to be picked up by extending arms.

2. One to four months
    a. waves bye-bye, plays pat-a-cake upon request.
    b. babbles or coos when spoken to or smiled at.
    c. TNR (tonic neck reflex) and stepping reflex disappear.

3. Four to eight months
    a. shows full attachment to mother or major caregiver.
    b. expresses emotions such as pleasure, anger and distress by making different kinds of sounds.
    c. sees outlines and shapes of nearby objects but cannot focus on distant objects.

4. Eight months to one year
    a. usually sleeps through the night.
    b. cuts several teeth.
    c. has a vocabulary of at least 50 words.

CHAPTER 5

The Toddler

TWELVE TO TWENTY-FOUR MONTHS

The toddler is a dynamo, full of unlimited energy and enthusiasm. While growth is reasonably uneventful during this stage, important changes are taking place in other developmental areas. The toddler period begins with the limited abilities of an infant and ends with the relatively sophisticated skills of a young child.

Improvements in motor skills allow toddlers to move about on their own, to explore, and test their surroundings. Rapid development of speech and language contributes to more complex thinking and learning abilities. Defiance and negative responses become commonplace near the end of this stage. Gradually, the toddler begins to assert independence as a way of gaining autonomy (a sense of self as separate and self-managed) and some degree of control over parents and caregivers.

THE ONE-YEAR-OLD

The ability to stand upright and toddle from place to place enables one-year-olds to gain new insight about their surroundings. They become talkers and doers, stopping only for much-needed meals and bedtimes. Their curiosity mounts, their skills become increasingly advanced, and their energy level seems never-ending. One-year-olds believe that everything and everyone exists for their benefit. Eventually, this egocentricity, or self-centeredness, gives way to a greater respect for others. However, for now, the one-year-old is satisfied to declare everything "mine" and to imitate the play and actions of other children rather than join in.

DEVELOPMENTAL PROFILES AND GROWTH PATTERNS

Growth and Physical Characteristics

- Rate of growth is considerably slower during this period.

Standing upright with support.

- Height increases approximately 2 to 3 inches (5.0–7.6 cm) per year to an average height of 32–35 inches (81.3–88.9 cm).
- Weights approximately 21–27 pounds (9.6–12.3 kg); gains $1/4$ to $1/2$ pound (0.13–0.25 kg) per month; weight is approximately three times the original birth weight.
- Respiration rate is typically 22–30 breaths per minute; varies with emotional state and activity.
- Heart beat (pulse) is approximately 80–110 per minute.
- Blood pressure is about 96/64.
- Head size increases slowly; grows approximately $1/2$ inch (1.3 cm) every six months; anterior fontanel is nearly closed at 18 months as bones of the skull thicken.
- Chest circumference is larger than head circumference.
- Rapid eruption of teeth; 6 to 10 new teeth will appear.
- Legs may still appear bowed.
- Body shape changes; takes on more adult-like appearance; still appears top heavy; abdomen protrudes, back is swayed.
- Visual acuity is approximately 20/60.

Motor Development

- Crawls skillfully and quickly.
- Stands alone with feet spread apart, legs stiffened, and arms extended for support.
- Gets to feet by self.
- Most children walk unassisted near the end of this period; falls often; not always able to maneuver around obstacles, such as furniture or toys.

- Uses furniture to lower self to floor; collapses backwards into a sitting position or falls forward on hands and then sits.
- Voluntarily releases an object.
- Enjoys pushing or pulling toys while walking.
- Repeatedly picks up objects and throws them; direction becomes more deliberate.
- Attempts to run; has difficulty stopping and usually just drops to the floor.
- Crawls up stairs on all fours; goes down stairs in same position.
- Carries toys from place to place.
- Enjoys crayons and markers for scribbling; uses whole-arm movement.
- Helps feed self; enjoys holding spoon and drinking from a glass or cup; not always accurate at getting utensils into mouth; frequent spills should be expected.
- Helps to turn pages in book.
- Stacks 2 to 4 objects.

Perceptual–Cognitive Development

- Enjoys object–hiding activities:
  –Early in this period, the child always searches in the same location for a hidden object (if child has watched the hiding of an object). Later, the child will search in several locations.
- Passes toy to other hand when offered a second object (referred to as "crossing the midline;" an important neurological development).
- Manages 3 to 4 objects by setting an object aside (on lap or floor) when presented with a new toy.

Enjoys looking at picture book and turning pages.

- Puts toys in mouth less often.
- Enjoys looking at picture books.
- Demonstrates understanding of functional relationships (objects that belong together):
  –Puts spoon in bowl and then uses spoon as if eating.
  –Places cup on saucer and sips from cup.
  –Tries to make doll stand up.
- Shows or offers toy for another person to look at.
- Names everyday objects.
- Places several small blocks in a container.
- Shows increasing understanding of spacial and form discrimination: puts all pegs in a six–peg board; places 3 geometric shapes in large form board or puzzle.
- Puts small items (clothespins, small cereal pieces) in a container or bottle and then dumps them out.
- Tries to make mechanical objects work after watching someone else do so.
- Responds with some facial movement, but cannot truly imitate facial expression.

Speech and Language Development

- Produces considerable "jargon": puts words and sounds together into speech–like (inflected) patterns.
- Holophrastic speech: one word conveys an entire thought; meaning depends upon the inflection.
- Follows simple directions, "Give daddy the cup."
- When asked, will point to familiar persons, animals, and toys.
- Identifies three body parts if someone names them: "Show me your nose (toe, ear)."
- Produces some two word phrases: "More cookie," "Daddy, bye–bye."
- Indicates a few desired objects and activities by name: "Bye–bye," "cookie"; verbal request is often accompanied by an insistent gesture.
- Responds to simple questions with "yes" or "no" and appropriate head movement.
- Speech is 25–50% **intelligible** during this period.
- Locates familiar objects on request (if child knows location of objects).
- Acquires and uses 5 to 50 words; typically these are words that refer to animals, food, and toys.

---

intelligible—Language is intelligible when it can be understood by others.

"Where's mommy's nose?"

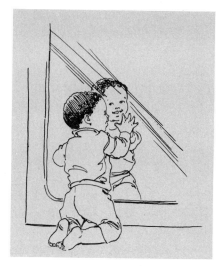

"Who's the pretty baby?"

- Uses gestures, such as pointing or pulling, to direct adult attention.
- Enjoys rhymes and songs; tries to join in.
- Seems aware of reciprocal (back and forth) aspects of conversational exchanges; some turn–taking in other kinds of vocal exchanges, such as making and imitating sounds.

Personal–Social Development

- Usually friendly toward others; becomes less wary of strangers.
- Helps pick up and put away toys.
- Plays alone for short periods.
- Enjoys being held and read to.
- Often imitates adult actions in play.
- Enjoys adult attention; likes to know that an adult is near.
- Recognizes self in mirror.
- Enjoys the companionship of other children but does not play co-operatively.
- Beginning to assert independence; often refuses to cooperate with daily routines that once were enjoyable; resists getting dressed, putting on shoes, eating, taking a bath; wants to try doing things without help.
- May have a tantrum when things go wrong or if overly tired or frustrated.
- Exceedingly curious about people and surroundings; needs to be watched carefully to prevent getting into dangerous situations.

DAILY ROUTINES—THE TODDLER (12–24 MONTHS)

Eating

- Has a decreased appetite; lunch is often the preferred meal of the day.
- Sometimes described as a finicky or fussy eater; may go on food jags; neither requires, nor wants, a large amount of food.
- Occasionally holds food in mouth without swallowing it; usually indicates child does not need or want any more to eat.
- Uses spoon with some degree of skill (if hungry and interested in eating).
- Has good control of cup: lifts it up, drinks from it, sets it down, holds with one hand.
- Helps feed self; some two-year-olds can feed self independently; others need help.

Bathing, Dressing, Toilet Needs

- Tries to wash self; plays with washcloth and soap.
- Takes off own shoes, stockings, some pants; attempts to dress self, often with little success: tries to put both feet into one pant leg, puts shirt on backwards or upside down.
- Helps when being dressed; puts arm in armhole, lifts feet to have socks put on.
- Lets parent or caregiver know when diaper or pants are soiled or wet.
- Begins to gain some control of bowels and bladder; complete control often not achieved until around age three. Bowel training can begin around twelve months; control is often achieved by eighteen months. Begins some bladder control after eighteen months.

Sleeping

- Falls asleep around 8 or 9 p.m.; however, will often fall asleep at dinner if nap has been missed.
- Makes many requests at bedtime for stuffed toys, a book or two, a special blanket.
- Has some problems going to sleep; overflow of energy shows itself in bouncing and jumping, calling for mother, demanding a drink, insisting on being taken to the bathroom, singing, making and remaking bed, all of which seems to be ways of "winding down."

Play and Social Activity

- Developing a strong sense of property rights; "mine" is heard frequently. Sharing is difficult, hoards toys and other items.
- Enjoys helping, but gets into "trouble" when left alone: smears toothpaste, tries on lipstick, empties dresser drawers.
- Enjoys talking about pictures; likes repetition, as in *Drummer Hoff, Mr. Bear, Dr. Seuss.*
- Enjoys walks; stops frequently to look at things (rocks, gum wrappers, insects); squats to examine them; much dawdling with no real interest in getting any place in particular.
- Still plays alone (solitary play) most of the time, though showing interest in other children, lots of watching; parallel play once in awhile but no cooperative play as yet (exception may be children who have spent considerable time in group care).
- At bedtime needs door left slightly ajar with light on in another room; seems to feel more secure, better able to settle down.
- Continues naps; naps too long or too late will interfere with bedtime.
- Wakes up slowly from nap; cannot be hurried or rushed into any activity at this time.

LEARNING ACTIVITIES

One-year-olds.

Tips for parents and caregivers.

- Respond to the toddler's jabbering and voice inflections, both in kind (playfully) and with simple words; maintain a conversational turn-taking.
- Encourage the toddler to point to familiar objects in picture books, catalogues, and magazines; name the objects and encourage the toddler to imitate (but do not insist).
- Hide a toy or other familiar object in an obvious place and encourage the toddler to find it (give clues as needed).
- Provide blocks, stacking rings, shape-sorting boxes, nesting cups; such toys promote problem-solving and eye-hand coordination.

- Allow water play frequently; the kitchen sink is always a favorite when an adult is working in the kitchen. (An old, absorbent throw rug will catch the spills and drips.)
- Put favorite toys in different parts of the room so the toddler must learn body navigation to get to them, by crawling, cruising, or walking (thus practicing motor skills, too).
- Provide toys that can be pushed and pulled, a stable plastic or wooden riding toy to steer that can be propelled with the feet; arrange safe, low places for climbing over, under, and on top of.

DEVELOPMENTAL ALERTS

Check with a health care provider or early childhood specialist if, by 24 months of age, the child *does not*:

- Attempt to talk or repeat words.
- Understand some new words.
- Respond to simple questions with "yes" or "no."
- Walk alone (or with very little help).
- Exhibit a variety of emotions: anger, delight, fear.
- Show interest in pictures.
- Recognize self in mirror.
- Attempt self-feeding: hold own cup to mouth and drink.

THE TWO-YEAR-OLD

This year can be a challenge—for the child, as well as for caregivers. Exasperated adults typically describe a two-year-old as "impossible" (or demanding, unreasonable, contrary). However, the two-year-old's fierce determination, tantrumming, and inability to accept limits are part of normal development and seldom under the child's control. The two-year-old faces demands that can be overwhelming: new skills and behaviors to be learned and remembered, learned responses to be perfected, and puzzling adult expectations with which to comply. Also, conflicting feelings of dependence and independence (autonomy) must be resolved. Is it any wonder that two-year-olds are frustrated, have difficulty making choices, and say no even to things they really want?

While this transitional year can be trying for all, good things also happen. Two-year-olds are noted for their frequent and spontaneous outbursts of laughter and affection. Also, as new skills are acquired and earlier learning is consolidated, the two-year-old gradually begins to function more ably and amiably.

Growth and Physical Development

- Weight gain averages 2 to 2.5 pounds (0.9–1.1 kg) per year; weighs approximately 26–32 pounds (11.8–14.5 kg) or about four times the weight at birth.
- Grows approximately 3–5 inches (7.6–12.7 cm) per year; average height is 34–38 inches (86.3–96.5 cm).
- Posture more erect; tummy still large and protruding, back swayed, due to abdominal muscles not yet fully developed.
- Respirations are slow and regular (approximately 20–35 breaths/minute).
- Body temperature continues to fluctuate with activity, emotional state, and environment.
- Brain reaches about 80% of its adult size.
- Eruption of teeth is nearly complete; second molars appear, for a total of 20 deciduous or "baby" teeth.

Motor Development

- Wide–stanced walk giving way to more erect, heel–to–toe pattern; able to maneuver around obstacles in pathway.
- Runs with greater confidence; has fewer falls.
- Squats for long periods while playing.
- Climbs stairs unassisted (but not with alternating feet).

With effort can balance on one foot.

Able to open doors.

- Balances on one foot (for a few moments), jumps up and down, but may still fall.
- Often achieves toilet training during this year (depending upon child's physical and neurological development); the child will indicate readiness.
- Throws a good-sized ball underhand without losing balance.
- Holds cup or glass (be sure it is unbreakable) in one hand.
- Unbuttons large buttons; unzips large zippers.
- Opens doors by turning doorknobs.
- Grasps large crayon with fist; scribbles enthusiastically.
- Climbs up on chair, turns around and sits down.
- Enjoys pouring and filling activities—sand, water.
- Stacks 4–6 objects on top on one another.
- Uses feet to propel wheeled riding toys.

Perceptual-Cognitive Development

- Eye-hand movements better coordinated; can put objects together, take them apart; fit large pegs into pegboard.
- Begins to use objects for purposes other than intended (may push a block around as a boat).
- Does simple classification tasks based on one dimension (separates toy dinosaurs from toy cars).
- Stares for long moments; seems fascinated by, or engrossed in, figuring out a situation at hand: where the tennis ball has rolled, where the dog has gone.

A scraped knee may result in a lot of tears.

- Attends to self–selected activities for longer periods of time.
- Discovering cause and effect: squeezes the cat makes her scratch.
- Knows where familiar persons should be; notes their absence; finds a hidden object by looking in last hiding place first.
- Names objects in picture books; may pretend to pick something off the page and taste or smell it.
- Recognizes and expresses pain and its location.

Speech and Language Development

- Enjoys being read to if allowed to participate by pointing, making relevant noises, turning pages.
- Realizes that language is effective for getting others to respond to needs and preferences.
- Uses 50 to 300 different words; vocabulary continuously increasing.
- Has broken the linguistic code; in other words, much of a two-year-old's talk has meaning to him or her.
- Receptive language more developed than expressive language; understands significantly more than they can talk about.
- Utters three- and four-word statements; uses conventional word order to form more complete sentences.
- Refers to self as "me" or sometimes "I" rather than by name, "Me go bye–bye"; has no trouble verbalizing "mine."
- Expresses negative statements by tacking on a negative word such as "no" or "not": "Not more milk."
- Repeatedly asks "What's that?"

- Uses some plurals; tells about objects and events not immediately present (this is both a cognitive and linguistic advance).
- Some stammering and other dysfluencies are common.
- Speech is as much as 65–70% intelligible.

Personal-Social Development

- Shows signs of empathy and caring: comforts another child who is hurt or frightened; sometimes is overly affectionate in offering hugs and kisses to children.
- Continues to use physical aggression if frustrated or angry (for some children, this is more exaggerated than for others); usually lessens as verbal skills improve.
- Temper tantrums likely to peak during this year; cannot be reasoned with while tantrum is in progress.
- Impatient; finds it difficult to wait or take turns.
- Enjoys "helping" with household chores; imitates everyday activities: may try to toilet a stuffed animal, feed a doll….
- "Bossy" with parents or primary caregiver; orders them about, makes demands, expects immediate compliance from adults.
- Watches and imitates the play of other children but seldom joins in; plays well alone.
- Offers toys to other children, but is usually possessive of playthings; tends to hoard toys.
- Making choices is difficult; wants it both ways.
- Often defiant; shouting "no" becomes nearly automatic.
- Ritualistic; wants everything "just so"; routines carried out exactly as before; belongings placed "where they belong."

May demonstrate care for a hurt friend.

Typically plays alone.

DAILY ROUTINES—TWO-YEAR-OLDS

Eating

- Appetite is fair; fluctuates with periods of growth; lunch is often the preferred meal.
- Sometimes described as a picky or fussy eater; often has strong likes and dislikes (which should be respected); may go on food jags (only eating certain foods such as peanut butter/jelly sandwiches, macaroni and cheese).
- Likes simple "recognizable" foods; dislikes mixtures; wants foods served in familiar ways.

"Look daddy, all clean!"

- May need between-meal snack; should be of good nutritive value, with "junk" foods unavailable.
- Increasingly able to feed self, but may be "too tired" to do so at times.
- Has good control of cup or glass, though spills happen often.
- Learns table manners by imitating adults and older children.

Sleeping

- Amount of nighttime sleep varies between 9 and 12 hours.
- Still requires afternoon nap; needs time to wake up slowly.
- May resist going to bed; usually complies if given ample warning and can depend on familiar bedtime routine (story, talk time, special toy).
- Takes awhile to fall asleep, especially if overly tired; may sing, talk to self, bounce on bed, call for parents, make and remake the bed (these seem to be ways of "winding down").

Bathing, Dressing, Toileting

- Enjoys bath if allowed ample playtime (*must never be left alone*); may object to being washed; tries to wash self.
- Usually dislikes, even resists, having hair washed.

- Tries to help when being dressed; needs simple, manageable clothing; can usually undress self.
- Shows signs of readiness for bowel training (some children may have already mastered bowel control).
- Stays dry for longer periods of time (one sign of readiness for toilet training); other signs may include interest in watching others use toilet, holding a doll or stuffed animal over toilet, clutching self, willingness to sit on potty for a few moments, expressing discomfort about being wet or soiled.

"I need to do potty."

Play and Social Activity

- Enjoys dressing up and imitating family activities: wearing father's hat makes child a "daddy".
- Likes to be around other children, but does not play well with them: observes them intently, imitating their actions (parallel play).
- Displays extreme negativism toward parents and caregivers—an early step toward establishing independence (autonomy).
- May have an imaginary friend as a constant companion.
- Explores everything in the environment, including other children; may shove or push other children as if to test their reaction.

LEARNING ACTIVITIES

Two-year-olds.

Tips for parents and caregivers.

- Share games such as lotto and picture dominoes that are based on matching colors, animals, facial expressions, everyday objects.
- Offer manipulative materials to foster problem-solving and eye-hand coordination: large beads for stringing, brightly colored cubes, puzzle boxes, the larger plastic interlocking bricks.

- Provide toy replicas of farm and zoo animals, families, cars, trucks, and planes for sorting and imaginative play.
- Read to the child regularly; provide colorful picture books for naming objects and describing everyday events; use simple illustrated story books, (one line per page) so the child can learn to tell or "read" the story.
- Share nursery rhymes, simple finger plays and action songs; respond to, imitate, and make up simple games based on the child's spontaneous rhyming or chanting.
- Set out (and keep a close eye on) washable paints, markers, chalk, large crayons and paper for artistic expression.
- Help with make-believe activities; example: save empty cereal boxes, discarded cans with intact labels for playing store.
- Provide wagons; large trucks and cars that can be loaded, pushed, or sat upon; doll carriage or stroller, a rocking boat; bean bags and rings for tossing.

DEVELOPMENTAL ALERTS

Check with a health care provider or early childhood specialist if, by the third birthday, the child *does not*:

- Eat a fairly well–rounded diet, even though amounts are limited.
- Walk confidently with few stumbles or falls.
- Avoid bumping into objects.
- Carry out simple two–step directions: "Come to Daddy and bring your book."
- Point to and name familiar objects: use two- or three-word sentences.
- Enjoy being read to.
- Show interest in other children: watching, perhaps imitating.
- Indicate a beginning interest in toilet training.
- Sort familiar objects according to a single characteristic, such as type, color, or size.

REVIEW QUESTIONS

1. Identify two motor skills that one- and two-year-olds typically acquire:
   a. one-year-old:

      1.

      2.

   b. two-year-old:

      1.

      2.

2. List three developmentally appropriate activities for a two-year-old (based on perceptual–cognitive and motor skills.
   a.

   b.

   c.

3. List three ways in which a one-year-old may begin to assert independence:
   a.

   b.

   c.

TRUE OR FALSE

1. A two-year-old can be expected to follow three–step instructions.

2. The ideal way to stop a temper tantrum is to pick the child up, set the child in a chair, and discuss the problem.

3. Parents should be concerned about their toddler who "doesn't seem to eat much."

4. Most two-year-olds have given up afternoon naps.

5. Toddlers should be punished for constantly getting into things.

6. Most two-year-olds can use language to make requests.

7. Children exhibit certain recognizable behaviors when they are ready to being toilet training.

8. Height and weight increases rapidly during this period.

MULTIPLE CHOICE. Select one or more correct answers from the lists below.

1. It is reasonable to expect most one-year-olds to
   a. use a spoon with full control.
   b. take off own shoes and stockings.
   c. catch a small ball.

2. Two-year-olds are most likely to engage in the type of play which is
   a. solitary.
   b. parallel.
   c. cooperative.

3. Caregivers should be concerned about the language development of a 2 ¹/₂ year old who consistently utters statements such as
   a. "No want mittens on."
   b. "Me go."
   c. "Shoes on right feets?"

4. Bedtime can be made easier by
   a. letting the child decide when and how bedtime should proceed.
   b. following the same basic routine every night.
   c. planning thirty minutes of vigorous activity before bedtime to make the child tired.

5. Changes in perceptual–cognitive development that occur between two and three years of age include the ability to
   a. take apart a stacking toy and put it back together.
   b. pull to a standing position.
   c. separate blocks into piles of red, yellow, blue.

CHAPTER 6

The Preschooler

Constant motion, eagerness, curiosity and joy of life characterize the healthy preschool-age child. During these years, abilities in all developmental areas undergo rapid change and expansion. Motor skills are being perfected. Creativity and imagination come into everything from dramatic play to art work to story-telling. Vocabulary and intellectual skills expand rapidly, allowing the child to express ideas, solve problems and plan ahead. Preschool children strongly believe in their own opinions. At the same time, they are developing some sense of the needs of others and some degree of control over their own behavior. Throughout the preschool years they strive for independence, yet they need continual reassurance that an adult is available to give assistance, to comfort or to rescue them if need be.

THE THREE-YEAR-OLD

DEVELOPMENTAL PROFILES AND GROWTH PATTERNS

Earlier conflicts, centered around struggles for independence, become fewer as children move through their third year of life. They are interested in cooperating and in accepting adult's directions. There is also an effort to delay gratification; in other words, they have less need to have what they want "right now." Furthermore, three-year-olds appear to love life. They have an irrepressible urge to find out about everything in their immediate world.

Growth and Physical Development

- Growth is slow and even.
- Height increases 2 to 3 inches (5–7.6 cm) per year; average height is 38 to 40 inches (96.5–101.6 cm) or nearly double the child's original birth length.
- Adult height can be predicted from measurements of height at 3 years of age; males are approximately 53% of their adult height, females 57%.

Appearance becomes more adult-like

- Gains 3 to 5 pounds (1.4–2.3 kg) per year; weighs an average of 30 to 38 pounds (13.6–17.2 kg).
- Heart rate (pulse) averages 90–110 beats per minute.
- Respiratory rate is 20–30 depending on activity level; child continues to breathe abdominally.
- Blood pressure reading is 84–90/60.
- Temperature reading averages 96 to 99.4 F. (35.5–37.4 C); is affected by activity, environmental conditions, and illness.
- Growth of legs is more rapid than arms giving the three-year-old a taller, thinner, adult-like appearance.

Walks up and down stairs using alternating feet

- Circumference of head and chest are equal; head-size is in better proportion to the rest of the body.
- Neck appears to lengthen as "baby fat" disappears.
- Posture is more erect; abdomen no longer protrudes and is smaller.
- Still appears slightly knock-kneed.
- Has a full set of "baby" teeth.
- Needs to consume approximately 1500 calories daily.
- Visual acuity is approximately 20/40 using the Snellen E chart.

Motor Development

- Walks up and down stairs independently, using alternating feet; may jump from bottom step, landing on both feet.
- Can balance momentarily on one foot.
- Kicks a large ball.
- Feeds self without assistance.
- Jumps in place.
- Pedals a small tricycle or wheeled toy.
- Throws a ball overhand.
- Catches a bounced ball with both arms extended.
- Enjoys swinging on a swing.
- Shows improved control of crayons or markers when drawing; uses vertical, horizontal and circular motions.
- Holds crayon or marker between first two fingers and thumb (tripod grasp), not in a fist as earlier.
- Turns pages of a book one at a time.

Kicks a large ball

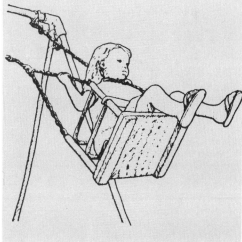

Enjoys swinging on a swing

Holds marker in tripod grasp   **Builds tower of eight or more blocks**

→ • Enjoys building with blocks.
  • Builds a tower of eight or more blocks.
→ • Enjoys playing with clay; pounds, rolls and squeezes it.

Washes and dries hands

- May begin to show preference for use of right or left hand.
- Carries a container of liquid, such as a cup of milk or bowl of water without much spilling; pours liquid from pitcher into another container.
- Manipulates large buttons and zippers on clothing.
- Washes and dries hands; brushes own teeth.
- Usually achieves complete bladder control during this time.

Perceptual and Cognitive Development

- Listens attentively to age-appropriate stories.
- Makes relevant comments during stories, especially to stories that relate to home and family events.
- Likes to look at books and may "read" to others or explain pictures.
- Enjoys stories with riddles, guessing and "suspense" (*The Noisy Book*).
- Points with 70% accuracy to correct pictures when given sound-alike words: *keys-cheese; fish-dish; mouse-mouth.*
- Enjoys story books that give real information; already boys are showing preference for stories about machinery.
- Plays realistically:
  —Feeds doll, puts it down for nap, covers it up.
  —Hooks truck and trailer together, loads truck, drives away making motor noises.
- Places 8 to 10 round pegs in beg board, or 6 round and 6 square blocks in form board.
- Attempts to draw, copies circles, squares, and some letters.

May "read" to others or explain pictures

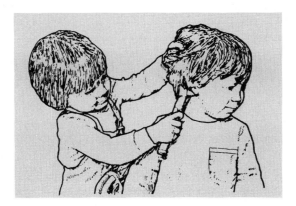

Plays realistically. Pretending to examine playmate's ear.

- Understands triangle, circle, square; can point to requested shape.
- Sorts objects logically on the basis of design, shape or color; however, chooses color or size predominantly as basis for classification.
- Shows understanding of basic size-shape comparisons 80% of the time; for example, will indicate which is bigger when shown tennis and golf balls; also understands smaller of the two.
- Names and matches primary colors: red, yellow, blue.
- Arranges cubes in horizontal line; also positions cubes to form a bridge.
- Estimates "how many" in sets of 1 to 4 and sometimes 1 to 5.
- Counts objects out loud.
- Chooses picture that has "more": cars, planes or kittens.

Enjoys attempting to reproduce circles and shapes

Imitates models of "trains" and "bridges"

• Shows some understanding of duration of time by using phrases such as "all the time," "all day," "for two days"; continued to show some confusion: "I didn't take a nap tomorrow."

Speech and Language Development

• Talks about known objects, events and people not present: "Jerry has a pool in his yard."
• Talks about the actions of others: "Daddy is mowing the grass."
• Adds information to what has just been said in a conversation: "Yeah, and then he grabbed it back."
• Answers simple questions appropriately.
• Asks increasing numbers of questions, particularly about location and identity of objects and people.
• Uses an increasing number of speech forms that keep conversation going: "What did he do next?"
• Calls attention to self, objects, or events in the environment: "Watch my helicopter fly."
• Promotes the behavior of others: "Let's jump in the water; You go first."
• Asks for desired objects or assistance.
• Joins in social interaction rituals: "Hi," "Bye," "Please."
• Comments about objects and ongoing events: "There's a house," "The tractor's pushing a boat."
• Vocabulary has grown to 300 to 1000 words.
• Recites nursery rhymes, sings songs.
• Speech is 80% intelligible.
• Produces expanded noun phrases: "...big, brown dog."
• Produces verbs with "ing" endings; uses "-s" to indicate more than one.

Counts out loud: 1, 2, 3, 4...

Answers questions about familiar objects and events

- Uses the preposition "in."
- Indicates negatives by inserting "no" or "not" before a simple noun or verb phrase, "Not baby."
- Answers "What are you doing?" "What is this?" and "Where?" questions dealing with familiar objects and events.

Personal-Social Development

- Seems to understand taking turns, but not always willing to do so.
- Friendly; laughs frequently; is eager to please.
- Occasional nightmares and fears of the dark, monsters or fire.
- Joins in simple games and group activities, sometimes hesitantly.
- Often talks to self.
- Uses objects symbolically in play; block of wood may be pushed as a truck, aimed as a gun, used as a ramp.
- Observes other children playing; may join in for a short time; often plays parallel to other children.
- Defends toys and other possessions; may become physically aggressive at times by grabbing a toy away, hitting another child, hiding toys.
- Engages in make-believe play alone and with other children.
- Shows affection toward children who are younger or children who get hurt.
- Sits and listens to stories up to ten minutes at a time; does not bother other children listening to story and resents being bothered.
- May continue to have a special security blanket, stuffed animal or toy for comfort.

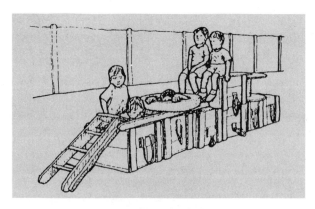

Engages in make-believe

DAILY ROUTINES—THREE-YEAR-OLDS

Eating

- Appetite fairly good; prefers small servings. Likes only a few cooked vegetables; eats almost everything else.
- Feeds self independently if hungry. Uses spoon in semi-adult fashion; may even spear with fork.
- Dawdles over food when not hungry.
- Can pour milk and juice and serve individual portions from a serving dish with some prompts ("Fill it up to the line"; "Take only two spoonsful."); fewer spills.
- Begins to drink a great deal of milk. (Must be sure child does not fill up on milk to the exclusion of other needed foods.)

Bathing, Dressing, Toileting

- Does a fair job of washing self in bath tub; still resists getting out of tub.
- Takes care of own toilet needs during the daytime (boys, especially, may continue to have pants-wetting accidents).
- Usually sleeps through the night without wetting the bed; some children are in transition—some days or even weeks they are dry, then may again experience night-wetting for a period.
- Child still more skilled at undressing than dressing self, though capable of putting on some articles of clothing.
- Becomes more skilled at manipulating buttons, large snaps, and zippers.

Sleeping

- Usually sleeps 10 to 12 hours at night, waking up about 7 or 8 a.m.; some children are awake much earlier.
- May no longer take an afternoon nap; continues to benefit from a quiet time on bed.
- Can get self ready for bed. Has given up many earlier bedtime rituals; may still need a bedtime story or song and tucking-in.
- May begin to have dreams that cause the child to awaken.
- Night wanderings may occur; quiet firmness is needed in returning child to his or her own bed.

Play and Social Activity

- The "me too" age; wants to be included in everything.
- Spontaneous group play for short periods of time; very social; beginning to play cooperatively.
- May engage in arguments with other children; adults should allow children to settle their own disagreements unless physical harm is threatened.
- Loves dress-up, dramatic play that involves every day work activities. Strong sex-role stereotypes: "Boys can't be nurses."
- Responds well to options rather than commands. "Do you want to put your nightgown on before or after the story?"
- Sharing still difficult, but seems to understand the concept.

LEARNING ACTIVITIES

Three-year-olds.

Tips for parents and caregivers.

- Allow the child to create new uses for everyday household items and discards: blanket over a table to make a cave; utensils for pretend cooking or cleaning; discarded mail for playing mail carrier; hose with small trickle of water for washing tricycle or wagon; oil can for servicing the vehicles.
- Provide somewhat more complex manipulative materials: parquetry blocks, peg boards with smaller pegs, various items to count, sort, and match; construction sets with medium-sized interlocking pieces.
- Offer non-toxic art and craft materials that encourage experimentation and creativity: crayons, washable markers, colored chalk, modeling clay, round-tipped scissors, papers, glue, paints and large brushes (supervision still required).
- Keep on hand a plentiful supply of books about animals, families, everyday events, alphabet and counting activities, poems and rhymes; continue daily reading sessions; encourage child to "read" to her- or himself.

- Provide three-wheeled tricycle or similar riding toys that build eye-hand-foot dexterity through steering and maneuvering; also, wheelbarrow and garden tools, doll stroller, shopping cart.
- Go for walks with the child, *at the child's pace;* allow ample time for child to explore, observe, and collect rocks, leaves, seed pods; name and talk about things along the way.

DEVELOPMENTAL ALERTS

Check with a health care provider or early childhood specialist if, by the fourth birthday, the child *does not*:

- Have intelligible speech most of the time.
- Understand and follow simple commands and directions.
- State own name and age.
- Enjoy playing near or with other children.
- Use 3 to 4 word sentences.
- Ask questions.
- Stay with an activity for 5 to 10 minutes.
- Jump in place without falling.
- Balance on one foot, at least briefly.
- Help with dressing self.

THE FOUR-YEAR-OLD

Four-year-olds are bundles of energy. They seem to be constantly engaged in non-stop activity. Bouts of stubbornness and arguments may be frequent between child and parent or caregiver. Children test limits in order to practice self-confidence and firm up a growing need for independence; many are loud, boisterous, even belligerent. They try adult's patience with their silly talk and silly jokes, their constant chatter and endless questions. At the same time, they have many lovable qualities. They are enthusiastic, try hard to be helpful, have lively imaginations, and can plan ahead to some extent: "When we get home, I'll make you a picture."

Affectionate toward younger children

DEVELOPMENTAL PROFILES AND GROWTH PATTERNS

Growth and Physical Characteristics

- Gains approximately 4 to 5 pounds (1.8–2.3 kg) per year; weighs an average of 32 to 40 pounds (14.5–18.2 kg).
- Grows 2 to 2.5 inches (5.0–6.4 cm) in height per year; is approximately 40 to 45 inches (101.6–114 cm) tall.
- Heart rate (pulse) averages 90–110 beats per minute.
- Respiratory rate ranges from 20–30 varying with activity and emotional level.
- Body temperature ranges from 98 to 99.4 F (36.6–37.4 C).
- Blood pressure remains at 84/60.
- Head circumference is usually not measured after age three.
- Requires approximately 1700 calories daily.
- Hearing acuity can be assessed by child's correct usage of sounds and language.
- Visual acuity is 20/30 as measured on the Snellen E chart.

Motor Development

- Walks on a straight line.
- Hops on one foot.
- Pedals and steers a tricycle or wheeled toy with confidence and skill; turns corners, avoids obstacles.

- Climbs ladders, steps, trees, playground equipment.
- Jumps over objects five or six inches high or from a step; lands with both feet together.
- Runs, starts, stops and moves around obstacles with ease.
- Throws a ball overhand.
- Builds a tower with 10 or more blocks using the dominant hand.
- Forms shapes and objects out of clay: cookies, snakes, animals.
- Reproduces some shapes and letters.
- Holds a crayon or marker using a tripod grasp.
- Paints and draws with deliberateness.
- Crosses legs when sitting on the floor.
- Becomes more accurate at hitting nails and pegs with hammer.
- Threads small wooden beads on a string.

Perceptual-Cognitive Development

- Stacks 5 graduated cubes from largest to smallest; builds a pyramid of 6 blocks.

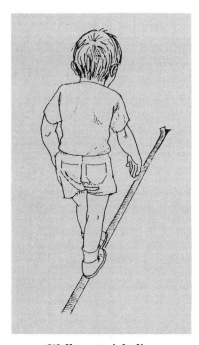

Walks a straight line

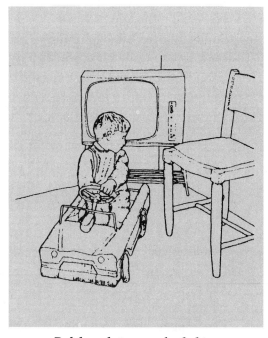

Pedals and steers a wheeled toy

Reproduces shapes and letters

- Can tell if paired words are the same or different in sound: *sheet/feet*, *ball/wall*.
- Places lower and upper case letters in form board.
- Near the end of this year, the child may: name about 75% of upper–case letters and write several; print own name; recognize some printed words (especially those which have a special meaning attached to them).
- Some children are beginning to read very simple books, such as alphabet books, with only a few words per page and many pictures.
- Likes stories about how things grow and how things operate.
- Delights in word play, creating silly language.
- Understands the concepts of "tallest," "biggest," "same," and "more"; selects the picture that has the "most houses" in it or the "biggest dogs."
- Identifies the number of pennies or chips from one to four by looking at the groups.
- Rote counts to 20 or more.
- Counts out a set of 1–7 objects from a larger group.
- Matches a set of 3 objects by pointing to the correct numeral.
- Understands the sequence of daily events: "When we get up in the morning, we get dressed, have breakfast, brush our teeth and go to school."
- Recognizes and identifies missing parts (of person, car, animal) in pictures.

Answers questions about "how many"

Speech and Language Development

- Uses the prepositions "on," "in," and "under."
- Uses possessives consistently: "hers," "theirs," "baby's."
- Uses "can't" and "don't" as well as "cannot" and "do not" to mark negatives.
- Answers "Whose?" "Who?" "Why?" and "How many?"
- Produces elaborate sentence structures: "The cat ran under the house before I could see what color it was."
- Speech is 95% intelligible.
- Begins to correctly use the past tense of verbs: "Mommy closed the door," "Daddy went to work."
- Refers to activities, events, objects, and people that are not currently present.
- Changes tone of voice and sentence structure to adapt to listener's level of understanding: To baby brother, "Milk gone?" To mother, "Did the baby drink all of his milk?"
- States first and last name, gender, siblings' names, and sometimes the telephone number.
- Answers appropriately when asked what to do if tired, cold, or hungry.
- Recites and sings simple songs and rhymes.

Personal-Social Development

- Outgoing; friendly; overly enthusiastic at times.
- Moods change rapidly and unpredictably; laughing one minute, crying the next; may throw tantrum over minor frustrations (a block structure that will not balance); sulk over being left out.
- Imaginary playmates or companions are common; holds conversations and shares strong emotions with this invisible friend.
- Boasts, exaggerates and "bends" the truth with made up stories or claims of boldness.
- Cooperates with others; participates in group activities.
- Shows pride in accomplishments; seeks frequent adult approval.
- Often appears selfish; not always able to take turns or to understand taking turns under some conditions.
- Tattles on other children.
- Demands doing many things independently, but may have a near-tantrum when problems arise: paint that drips, paper airplane that will not fold right.
- Enjoys role-playing and make-believe activities.
- Relies (most of the time) on verbal rather than physical aggression; may yell angrily rather than hitting to make a point.
- Name-calling and taunting are ways of excluding other children.
- Establishes close friendships with playmates; beginning to have a "best" friend.

Cooperates with others   Takes pride in accomplishments

DAILY ROUTINES—FOUR-YEAR-OLDS

Eating

- Appetite fluctuates from very good to fair.
- May develop dislikes of certain foods and refuse them to the point of tears if pushed.
- Uses all eating utensils; becomes quite skilled at spreading jelly or peanut butter or cutting soft foods such as bread.
- Eating and talking get in each other's way; talking usually takes precedence over eating.
- Likes to help in the preparation of a meal; dumping premeasured ingredients, washing vegetables, setting the table.

Bathing, Dressing, Toileting

- Takes care of own toileting needs; often demands privacy in the bathroom.
- Does an acceptable job of bathing and brushing teeth, but should receive assistance (or subtle inspection) from adults on a regular basis.
- Dresses self, can lace shoes, button buttons, buckle belts. Gets frustrated if problems arise in getting dressed and may stubbornly refuse much-needed adult help.
- Can sort and fold own clean clothes, put clothes away, hang up towels, straighten room.

Sleeping

- Averages 10 to 12 hours of sleep at night; may still take an afternoon nap or quiet time.
- Bedtime usually not a problem if cues, rather than parents' orders, signal the command: when the story is finished, when the clock hands are in a certain position.
- Some children fear the dark, but usually a light left on in the hall is all that is needed.
- Getting up to use a toilet may require helping the child settle down for sleep again.

Play and Social Activities

- Playmates are important; plays cooperatively most of the time; may be bossy.
- Takes turns; shares (most of the time); wants to be with children every waking moment.
- Needs (and seeks out) adult approval and attention; may comment, "Look what I did."
- Understands and needs limits (but not too constraining); will abide by rules most of the time.
- Brags about possessions; shows off; boasts about family members.

LEARNING ACTIVITIES

Four-year-olds.

Tips for parents and caregivers.

- Join in simple board and card games that depend on chance, not strategy; emphasis should be on playing, not winning. (Learning to be a good sport does not come until much later in childhood.)
- Provide puzzles with five to ten pieces (number of pieces depends upon the child), counting and alphabet games, matching games such as more detailed lotto.
- Offer various kinds of simple scientific and math materials: ruler, compass, magnifying glass, simple scales; activities such as collecting grasses, growing worms, sprouting seeds.
- Appreciate (and sometimes join in) the child's spontaneous rhyming, chanting, silly name-calling, jokes, riddles.
- Continue daily read-aloud times; encourage the child to supply words or phrases, to guess *what comes next.* to retell the story (or parts of it); introduce the idea of "looking things up" in a simple picture dictionary or encyclopedia; go to the library regularly, allowing the child ample time to choose books.
- Encourage all kinds of vigorous outdoor activity; water play in sprinkler or plastic pool (*pool requires adult presence*); offer unpressured swimming, tumbling, or dancing lessons.

DEVELOPMENTAL ALERTS

Check with a health care provider or early childhood specialist if, by the fifth birthday, the child *does not*:

- State own name in full.
- Recognize simple shapes: circle, square, triangle.
- Catch a large bounced ball.
- Speak so as to be understandable to strangers.
- Have good control of posture and movement.
- Hop on one foot.
- Appear interested in and responsive to surroundings.
- Respond to statements without constantly asking to have them repeated.
- Dress self with minimal adult assistance; manage buttons, zippers.
- Take care of own toileting needs; have good bowel and bladder control with infrequent accidents.

THE FIVE-YEAR-OLD

Five-year-old children are in a period of relative calm. There is greater emotional control. The child is friendly and outgoing much of the time, and is becoming self-confident and reliable. The world is expanding beyond home and family and child-care center. Friendships and group activities are of major importance at this age.

Constant practice and mastery of skills in all areas of development is the major focus of the five-year-old. However, this quest for mastery coupled with a high energy level and robust self-confidence can lead to mishap. Eagerness to do and explore often interferes with the ability to foresee danger or potentially disastrous consequences of their own behavior. Therefore, the child's safety and the prevention of accidents must be a major concern of parents and caregivers. At the same time, adults' concerns must be handled in ways that do not interfere with the child's development.

DEVELOPMENTAL PROFILES AND GROWTH PATTERNS

Growth and Physical Characteristics

- Gains 4 to 5 pounds (1.8–2.3 kg) per year; weighs an average of 38 to 45 pounds (17.3–20.5 kg).
- Grows an average of 2 to 2.5 inches (5.1–6.4 cm) per year; is approximately 42 to 46 inches (106.7–116.8 cm) tall.
- Heart rate (pulse) is approximately 90–110 beats per minute.
- Respiratory rate ranges from 20–30 depending on activity and emotional status.
- Body temperature is stabilized at 98 to 99.4 F.
- Head size is approximately that of an adult's.
- May begin to lose "baby" (deciduous) teeth.
- Body is adult-like in proportion.
- Requires approximately 1800 calories daily.
- Visual acuity is 20/20 using the Snellen E chart.
- Visual tracking and binocular vision are well-developed.

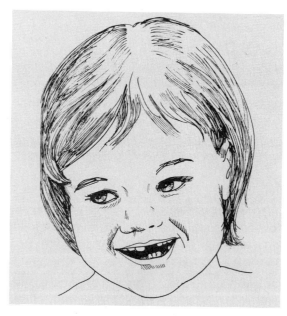

Begins to lose teeth

Walks across a balance beam

Balances on either foot

Motor Development

- Walks backwards, heel to toe.
- Walks unassisted up and down stairs, alternating feet.
- May learn to turn somersaults (should be taught the right way in order to avoid injury).

Builds structures from models

Cuts on the line with scissors

- Bends to touch toes without flexing knees.
- Walks a balance beam.
- Learns to skip using alternating feet.
- Catches a ball thrown from three feet away.
- Rides a tricycle or wheeled toy with speed and skillful steering; some children learning to ride bicycles.
- Jumps or hops forward on both feet ten times in a row without falling.
- Balances on either foot with good control for ten seconds.
- Builds three dimensional structures with small cubes by copying from a picture or model.
- Reproduces many shapes and letters: square, triangle, *A, I, O, U, C, H, L, T, V.*
- Demonstrates good control of pencil or marker; may begin to color within the lines.
- Cuts on the line with scissors (not perfectly).
- Hand dominance is usually established.

Perceptual and Cognitive Development

- Forms rectangle from two triangular cuts.
- Builds steps with set of small blocks.
- Understands concept of same shape, same size.
- Sorts objects on the basis of both color and form.

- Sorts a variety of objects in such a say that all things in the group have a single common feature (classification skill: all are food items or boats or animals).
- Does not yet recognize class inclusion: that is, when given a set of wooden beads with many red ones, a few blue ones, child can understand that all beads are wooden and some are red and some are blue, but when asked "Are there more red beads or more wooden beads?" the child replies, "More red ones."
- Understands the concepts of smallest and shortest; places objects in order from shortest to tallest, smallest to largest.
- Identifies objects with specified serial position: first, second, last.
- Rote counts to twenty and above.
- Recognizes numerals from one to ten.
- Understands the concepts of less than, "Which bowl has less water?"
- Understands the terms dark, light, and early: "I got up early, before anyone else. It was still dark."
- Relates clock time to daily schedule: "It is time to turn on TV when the clock hands point to 5."
- Some children can tell time on the hour: five o'clock, two o'clock.
- Knows what a calendar is for.
- Recognizes and identifies penny, nickel and dime.

Identifies and names at least four colors

Participates in elaborate make-believe

- Understands the concept of one-half; can say how many pieces an object has when its been cut in half.
- Continues to ask many questions.
- Eager to learn new things.

Speech and Language Development

- Vocabulary of 1500 words or more.
- Tells a familiar story while looking at pictures in a book.
- Defines simple words by function: a ball is to bounce; a bed is to sleep in.
- Identifies and names at least four colors.
- Recognizes the humor in simple jokes; makes up jokes and riddles.
- Produces sentences with an average length of 5 to 7 words.
- States the name of own city and town, birthday, and parents' names.
- Answers telephone appropriately; calls person to phone or takes a brief message.
- Speech is nearly 100% intelligible.
- Uses "would" and "could" appropriately.
- Uses past irregular verbs consistently: "went," "caught," "swam," "gave."
- Uses past tense inflection (-ed) appropriately to mark regular verbs: "jumped," "rained," "washed."
- Understands the singular/plural contrast for nouns: *ball/balls, block/blocks, baby/babies.*

Personal-Social Development

- Enjoys friendships; often has one or two special playmates.
- Is often generous: shares toys, takes turns, plays cooperatively; has occasional lapses.
- Participates in group play and shared activities with the other children; suggests imaginative and elaborate play ideas.
- Is affectionate and caring, especially toward younger or injured children and animals.
- Generally does what parent or caregiver requests; follows directions and carries out responsibilities most of the time.
- Continues to need adult comfort and reassurance but may be less open in seeking and accepting comfort.
- Has better self-control; has fewer dramatic swings of emotions.
- Like to tell jokes, entertain and make people laugh.
- Boastful about accomplishments.

DAILY ROUTINES—FIVE-YEAR-OLDS

Eating

- Eats well, but not at every meal.
- Likes familiar foods, prefers most vegetables raw.
- Often adopts food dislikes of family members and caregivers.
- Makes breakfast (pours cereal, gets out milk and juice) and lunch (spreads peanut butter and jam on bread).

Bathing, Dressing, Toileting

- Takes full responsibility for own toileting; may put off going to the bathroom until an accident occurs or is barely avoided.
- Bathes fairly independently but needs some help getting started.
- Dresses self completely; learning to tie shoes, sometimes aware when clothing is on wrong side out or backwards.
- Careless with clothes; leaves them strewn about; needs many reminders to pick them up.
- Uses tissue for blowing nose, but often does a careless or incomplete job; forgets to throw it away.

Sleeping

- Independently manages all routines associated with getting ready for bed; can help with younger brother or sister's bedtime routine.
- Averages 10 or 11 hours of sleep per night. The occasional 5-year-old still naps.
- Dreams and nightmares are commonplace.
- Going to sleep is often delayed if the day has been especially exciting or exciting events are scheduled for the next day.

Play and Social Activities

- Helpful and cooperative in carrying out family chores and routines.
- Somewhat rigid about the "right" way to do something and the "right" answers to a question.
- Fearful that mother may not come back; very attached to home and family; willing to adventure to some degree but wants the adventure to begin and end at home.
- Plays well with other children, but three may be a crowd: two 5-year-olds will often exclude the third.
- Shows affection and protection toward younger sister or brother, may feel overburdened at times if younger child demands too much attention.

LEARNING ACTIVITIES

Five-year-olds.

Tips for parents and caregivers.

- Provide inexpensive materials (computer paper, wall paper books, paint samples, scraps of fabric) for cutting, pasting, painting, coloring, folding; also, offer such things as simple looms for weaving, simple sewing activities, smaller beads for stringing; wood scraps and tools for simple carpentry.
- Continue to collect props and dress-up clothes that allow more detailed acting out of family and worker roles; visit and talk about community activities—house building, post office and mail pickups, farmers' market; encourage play with puppets; assist in creating a stage (a cut out carton works well).
- Use a variety of books to help the child learn to access the many joys and functions of books in everyday life; continue to read aloud, regularly and frequently.
- Encourage the growing interest in paper and pencil games and number, letter, and word recognition games which the child often invents but may need adult help in carrying out.
- Plan actual cooking experiences that allow the child to chop vegetables, roll out cookies, measure, mix, and stir.
- Help set up improvised target games that promote eye-hand coordination: bean bag toss, bowling, ring toss, low hoop and basketball; ensure opportunities for vigorous play: wheel toys; jungle gyms and parallel bars; digging, raking, hauling.

DEVELOPMENTAL ALERTS

Check with a health care provider or early childhood specialist if, by the sixth birthday, the child *does not*:

- Alternate feet when walking down stairs.
- Speak in a moderate voice; neither too loud, too soft, too high, too low nor monotone.
- Sometimes follows a series of 3 directions in order ("Stop, pick up the cup and bring it here").

- Use 4 to 5 words in acceptable sentence structure.
- Cut on a line with scissors.
- Sit still and listen to an entire short story (5 to 7 minutes).
- Maintain eye contact when spoken to (unless this is a cultural taboo).
- Play well with other children.
- Perform most self-grooming tasks independently: brush teeth; wash hands and face.

REVIEW QUESTIONS

1. List three motor skills that appear between 2 and 5 years of age.
   a.

   b.

   c.

2. List a social/personal skill typical of each of the following ages.
   a. 3 year olds:

   b. 4 year olds:

   c. 5 year olds:

3. List three major speech and language skills in order of their appearance that develop between 3 and 5 years of age.
   a.

   b.

   c.

TRUE OR FALSE

1. Growth is slow and even during most of the preschool years.

2. A full set of baby teeth is usually in place by 3 or 4 years of age.

3. Complete bladder control is achieved between 3 and 5 years of age.

4. 15 to 18 hours of sleep at night is characteristic of the older preschool age child.

5. Silly talk and silly jokes (that is, silly to adults) seem to go hand in hand with the development of language skills in the preschool age child.

6. Imaginary playmates are common among preschool age children.

7. Fluctuations in appetite are perfectly normal during the preschool years.

8. Safety and prevention of accidents need not concern adults because preschool-age children have learned to be cautious.

9. It is most unusual for 5-year-olds to have dreams or nightmares.

10. Defining nouns by function (what the object does) is characteristic of the older preschool age child: "A kite is to fly." "A book is to read."

MULTIPLE CHOICE. Select one or more correct answers from the list below.

1. Which of the following might be cause for concern if a three-year-old were not doing them?
   a. talking clearly enough to be understood most of the time
   b. stating own name
   c. using scissors to cut out shapes accurately

2. Which of the following might be of concern if a four-year-old were not doing them?
   a. hopping on one foot
   b. printing all letters of the alphabet legibly and in order
   c. dressing self with only occasional help from the parent or caregiver

3. Which of the following might be cause for concern if a child were not doing them by age five?
   a. listening to a story for 5 minutes
   b. making an acceptable sentence using 4 or 5 words
   c. alternating feet when walking down stairs

4. Which of the following describe most healthy preschool age children?
   a. eager to find out all about everything they contact
   b. vocabulary and intellectual skills are expanding rapidly
   c. content to stay close to adults; not willing to begin to branch out into activities with other children

5. Which of the following expectations are unrealistic of preschool age children?
   a. explaining why they did something unacceptable
   b. being responsible for younger brothers and sisters
   c. answering the telephone pleasantly

CHAPTER 7

School Age Children

SIX-, SEVEN-, AND EIGHT-YEAR-OLDS

The period following the preschool years is especially remarkable. Children appear to be in a stage of developmental integration; they are gradually organizing and combining various developmental skills so they can achieve increasingly complex tasks. At this age, boys and girls alike are becoming competent at taking care of their own personal needs—washing, dressing, toileting, eating, getting up and getting ready for school. They observe family rules about mealtimes, television, and needs for privacy. They can also be trusted to run errands and carry out simple responsibilities at home and school. In other words, these are children in control of themselves and their immediate world.

Will understand rules about watching television.

"I love the smell of roses."

Above all, six-, seven- and eight-year-olds are ready and eager to go to school, even though they may become somewhat apprehensive when the time actually arrives. Going to school creates anxieties, such as arriving on time, remembering to bring back assigned items, and walking home alone or to after–school child care.

Learning to read is the most complex perceptual task the child encounters following the preschool years. It involves recognizing the visual letter symbols and associating them with their spoken sound. It also means that children must learn to combine letters to form words and to put these words together into intelligible thoughts that can be read or spoken. Yet, complex as the task is, most children between six and eight years of age become so adept at reading that the skill is soon taken for granted.

Sensory activities are essential to all learning in young children. Developmental kindergartens and primary classes recognize this. They emphasize sensory experiences by encouraging children to manipulate many kinds of materials—blocks, puzzles; paints; glue, paper, and found materials; sand and water and dirt; musical instruments and measurement devices. They also provide many opportunities for projects such as cooking, gardening, carpentry, and dramatic play. The hands-on approach to the education of six-, seven-, and eight-year-olds, as well as younger children, is strongly endorsed by NAEYC (National Association for the Education of Young Children). The philosophy is clearly presented in what has come to be called Developmentally Appropriate Practices, NAEYC's publication, *Developmentally Appropriate Practices in Early Childhood Programs Serving Children from Birth through Eight.*

Play continues to be one of the most important activities for fostering cognitive development in the early grades. It is also a major route to enhancing social development and all other developmental skills. For the most part, six-, seven-, and eight-year olds play well with other children, especially if the group is not too large and children are of a similar age. There is a keen interest in making friends, being a friend, and having friends. At the same time, they also may do a good deal of tattling, quarreling, bossing, and excluding: "If you play with Lynette, then you're not *my* friend." Some children show considerable aggression but it often tends to be more verbal than physical, aimed at hurting other's feelings rather than causing physical harm.

Friends are usually playmates that the child has ready access to in the neighborhood and at school. Friends are often defined as someone who is "fun," "pretty," "strong," or who "acts nice." However, friendships at this age are easily established and readily abandoned, few are stable or long–lasting.

Throughout the early school years, many children seem almost driven by the need to do everything right. On the other hand, they enjoy being challenged and completing tasks. They also like to make recognizable products and to join in organized activities. Overall, most children enjoy the early school years. They become quite comfortable with themselves, their parents, and their teachers.

School-age children generally play well together.

THE SIX-YEAR-OLD

New and exciting adventures begin to open up to six-year-olds as their coordination improves and their size and strength increase. However, new challenges are often met with a mixture of enthusiasm and frustration. Six-year-olds typically set unrealistically high standards for themselves, have difficulty making choices, and, at times, are overwhelmed by unfamiliar situations. At the same time, changes in their cognitive abilities enable them to see that underlying rules are often useful for understanding everyday events, objects, and the behavior of others.

For many children, this period also marks the beginning of formal, subject–oriented schooling (it should be noted that formal, academic learning activities are considered developmentally inappropriate by many early childhood educators). Behavior problems or signs of tension, such as tics, nail–biting, or bed–wetting may flair up. Generally these pass as children become familiar with new expectations and responsibilities associated with going to school. Despite the turmoil and trying times (for adults as well), most six-year-olds experience an abundance of good times marked by a lively curiosity, an eagerness to learn, an endearing sense of humor, and exuberant outbursts of affection and good will.

DEVELOPMENTAL PROFILES AND GROWTH PATTERNS

Growth and Physical Characteristics

- Growth occurs slowly, but steadily.
- Height increases 2–3 inches (5–7.5 cm) each year; girls are an average of 42–46 inches (105–115 cm) tall, boys, 44–47 inches (110–117.5 cm).
- Weight increases 5–7 pounds (2.3–3.2 kg) a year: girls weigh approximately 38–47 pounds (19.1–22.3 kg), boys, 42–49 pounds (17.3–21.4 kg).
- Weight gains reflect significant increases in muscle mass.
- Heart rate (80 beats/minute) and respiratory rates (18–28 breaths/minute) are similar to those of adults; rates vary with activity.
- Body takes on a lanky appearance as long bones of the arms and legs begin a phase of rapid growth.
- Loses "baby" (deciduous) teeth; permanent (secondary) teeth erupt, beginning with the two upper front teeth; girls tend to lose teeth at an earlier age than boys.
- Visual acuity should be 20/20; children testing 20/40 or less should have a professional evaluation.
- Farsightedness is not uncommon; often due to immature development (shape) of the eyeball.
- Facial features become more adult–like.
- Requires approximately 1600–1700 calories per day.

Motor Development

- Muscle strength increases; typically, boys are stronger than girls of similar size.
- Gain greater control over large and fine motor movements; movements are more precise and deliberate, though some clumsiness persists.
- Enjoys vigorous physical activity: running, jumping, climbing, and throwing.
- Moves constantly even when trying to sit still.
- Increasing dexterity and eye-hand coordination along with improved motor functioning which facilitates learning to ride a bicycle, swim, swing a bat, or kick a ball.
- Enjoys art projects: likes to paint, model with clay, "make things," draw and color, work with wood.
- Writes numbers and letters with varying degrees of precision and interest; some children continue to reverse or confuse certain letters: b/d, p/g, g/q, t/f.
- Traces around hand and other objects.
- Folds and cuts paper in simple shapes.
- Ties own shoes.

Learning to ride a bicycle is a major event in a child's life.

**There is the same amount of water
in each jar.**

Perceptual and Cognitive Development

- Span of attention increases; works at tasks for longer periods of time, though concentrated effort is not always consistent.
- Understands a few abstract concepts such as simple time markers (today, tomorrow, yesterday); or uncomplicated concepts of motion (cars go faster than bicycles).
- Begins to understand elementary principles of conservation: while jars that are tall and narrow may look different than those that are short and wide, they may hold the same amount.
- Recognizes seasons and major holidays and the activities associated with each.
- Enjoys the challenge of puzzles, counting and sorting activities, paper and pencil mazes, and games that involve matching letters and words with pictures.
- Recognizes some words by sight; attempts to sound out printed words (some children may be reading well by this time).
- Identifies familiar coins: pennies, nickels, dimes, quarters.
- Can hold up and correctly name right and left hands.
- Clings to certain beliefs involving magic or fantasy; the Tooth Fairy swapping a coin for a tooth; Santa Claus bringing gifts.
- Arrives at some understanding about death and dying; often expresses fear that parents may die, especially mother.

"This is my left hand."

Speech and Language Development

- Loves to talk, often nonstop; may be described as a chatterbox.
- Able to carry on adult–like conversations; asks many question.

Enjoys jokes and laughing.

- Learns as many as 5 to 10 new words each day; vocabulary consists of 10,000 to 14,000 words.
- Uses appropriate verb tenses, word order, and sentence structure.
- Increasingly uses language, rather than tantrums or physical aggression, to express displeasure: "That's mine! Give it back, you dummy."
- Talks self through steps required in simple problem–solving situations (though the "logic" may be unclear to adults).
- Imitates slang and profanity; finds "bathroom talk" extremely funny.
- Delights in telling jokes and riddles; often, the humor is far from subtle.
- Enjoys being read to and making up stories.
- Capable of learning more than one language; does so spontaneously in a bi– or multi–lingual family.

Personal-Social Development

- Experiences sudden mood swings: may be "best of friends" one minute, "worst of enemies" the next; loving one day, uncooperative and irritable the next; is especially unpredictable toward mother or principal caregiver.
- Becoming less dependent on parents as friendship circle expands; still desires some closeness and nurturing, yet has urges to break away and "grow up."
- Makes friends easily, but not always good at keeping them.
- Anxious to please; needs and seeks adult approval, reassurance, and praise; may complain excessively about minor hurts to gain more attention.
- Continues to be self–centered (egocentric); still sees events almost entirely from own perspective: views everything and everyone as there for child's own benefit.
- Easily disappointed and frustrated by self–perceived failure; intolerate of own imperfections.
- Cannot tolerate being corrected or losing at games; often goes "all to pieces": may sulk, cry, refuse to play, or reinvent rules to suit own purpose.
- Enthusiastic and inquisitive about surroundings and everyday events.
- Little or no understanding of ethical behavior or moral standards; often fibs, cheats, or "steals" objects belonging to others.
- Tries to be good; knows when he or she has been "bad"; values of "good" and "bad" are based on expectations and rules of parents and teachers.
- May be increasingly fearful of thunderstorms, the dark, unidentified noises, dogs and other animals.

DAILY ROUTINES—SIX YEAR OLDS

Eating

- Has a good appetite most of the time; often takes larger helpings than is able to finish. May skip an occasional meal, but usually makes up for it later.

- Willingness to try new foods is unpredictable; has strong food preferences and definite dislikes.

- Table manners often seem deplorable by adult standards; may revert to eating with fingers; stuff mouth; continues to spill milk or drop food in lap.

- Has difficulty using table knife for cutting and fork for anything but spearing food.

- Finds it difficult to sit through an entire meal; wiggles and squirms, gets off (or "falls" off) chair, drops utensils.

Bathing, Dressing, Toileting

- Balks at having to take a bath; finds many excuses for delaying or avoiding a bath entirely.

- Manages toileting routines without much help; sometimes is in a hurry or waits too long so that "accidents" happen.

- May revert to soiling or wetting pants during the first few weeks of school.

- Usually sleeps through the night without having to get up to use the bathroom. NOTE: some children (especially boys) may not be able to maintain a dry bed for another year or so.

Forgetful about caring for clothing.

- Careless about handwashing, bathing, and other self–care routines; needs frequent supervision and demonstration of skills to make sure they are carried out properly.
- Interested in selecting own clothes; needs subtle guidance in determining combinations and seasonal appropriateness.
- Drops clothing on floor or bed, loses shoes around the house, flings jacket down and often forgets where it is.

Sleep

- Continues to need 9–11 hours of uninterrupted sleep.
- Usually sleeps through the night; some children continue to have nightmares.
- May need night-light, special blanket, or favorite stuffed toy (sometimes all three).
- Finds numerous ways to avoid bedtime; when finally in bed, falls asleep quickly.
- If awake before parents, usually finds ways to amuse self with books, toys, or coloring.

Play and Social Activities

- Strong sense of self is evident in terms of preferences and dislikes; uncompromising about wants and needs (often these do not coincide with adult plans or desires).
- Possessive about toys and books, parents and friends, but is increasingly able to share.
- May have close, friendly relationship with one or two other children (often slightly older); play involves working together toward specific goals.
- Intolerant of being told what to do; may revert to tantrums.
- Eager for teacher's attention, praise, reassurance; now views teacher (rather than parent) as the ultimate source of "truth."

LEARNING ACTIVITIES

Six-year-olds.

Tips for parents and caregivers.

- Provide materials for coloring, cutting, pasting, painting (paper chains are always big, regardless of the season).
- Offer paper and pencil games: dot-to-dot, number-to-number, find-the-imbedded-items; copying and tracing activities.
- Provide (and frequently join in) simple card and board games, especially those where competitiveness can be played down.
- Keep a plentiful supply of books on hand for the child to read and look at as well as for the adult to read to the child.
- Allow collecting of objects according to child's own interest and system (which may make little sense to the adult).
- Make interesting dress-up clothes available for boys as well as girls; encourage housekeeping play and role-playing: teacher, pilot, hunter, plumber, doctor (needs constant supervision).
- Encourage simple cookery, carpentry, and construction activities with construction sets, blocks, cars, trucks, planes, zoo, and farm animals. (For the most part it is best to avoid battery driven and other mechanical toys—once the novelty has worn off they offer little involvement, hence little learning).
- Encourage bicycling, roller skating, swimming, experimenting on monkey bars; digging, throwing, catching, and batting activities.

DEVELOPMENTAL ALERTS

Check with a health care provider or early childhood specialist if, by the seventh birthday, the child *does not*:

- Show signs of ongoing growth: increasing height and weight; continuing motor development, such as running, jumping, balancing.
- Show some interest in reading and trying to reproduce letters, especially own name.
- Follow simple, multiple–step directions: "Finish your book, put it on the shelf, and then get your coat on."

- Follow through with instructions and complete simple tasks: putting dishes in the sink, picking up clothes, finishing a puzzle. NOTE: All children forget. Task incompletion is seldom a problem unless a child repeatedly leaves tasks unfinished.
- Begin to develop alternatives to excessive use of inappropriate behaviors in order to get own way.
- Develop a steady decrease in tension–type behaviors that may have developed with starting school: repeated grimacing or facial tics; eye twitching; grinding of teeth; regressive soiling or wetting; frequent stomachaches; refusing to go to school.

THE SEVEN- AND EIGHT-YEAR-OLD

Seven- and eight-year-olds continue to grow slowly, but steadily, and to improve many skills. Opportunities for spending more time away from home, playing at a friend's house, participating in organized groups and activities, or riding bikes around the neighborhood broaden this age group's knowledge of the world. These children can be trusted to carry out instructions, and they enjoy responsibilities, such as caring for a family pet, watching a sibling while a parent is busy, or helping to rake the yard. Friendships are important, easily established, readily abandoned, and seldom stable or long–lasting. Seven- and eight-year-olds continue to show strong sex–role stereotypes: "Mommies can't be pilot," "Men can't be nurses". Play is still important for fostering children's social development, refining their basic motor skills, and contributing to their self–esteem.

DEVELOPMENTAL PROFILES AND GROWTH PATTERNS

Growth and Physical Characteristics

- Weight gains continue to average 5–7 pounds (2.3–3.2 kg) per year; an eight-year-old weighs approximately 55–61 pounds (25–27.7 kg). Girls typically gain less weight than boys.
- Height increases 2.5 inches (6.25 cm) per year on the average; girls measure 46–49 inches (115–122.5 cm), boys 48–52 inches (120–130 cm); girls tend to grow taller than boys.

Enjoys competitive activities.

- Assume a tall, thin, lanky appearance as arms and legs grow longer.
- Respiratory (16–30 breaths/minute) and heart rate (70–75 beats/minute) reflect more adult-like patterns, although they vary with activity.
- Eyeballs continue to change shape and size; vision should be checked periodically to ensure good sight.
- Hair often grows darker in color.
- Posture becomes straighter and more erect.
- Baby teeth continue to be replaced with permanent teeth.
- Frequency of minor illnesses decreases.

Motor Development

- Participates enthusiastically in competitive activities.
- Likes to dance, roller skate, swim, run, wrestle, and play ball games such as soccer, baseball, and kickball.
- Exhibits significant improvement in agility, balance, control of motor abilities, and endurance; can balance on one foot, jump rope, and play catch.
- Seven-year-olds maintain tight hold on pencil; grip and movements are generally less tense by age 8.
- Produces letters and numbers in a deliberate and confident fashion: characters are increasingly uniform in size and shape; may run out of room on line or page when writing.

May recognize the value of money.

- Uses knife and fork to cut food.
- Practices new skills over and over in order to perfect them.

Perceptual and Cognitive Development

- Collects objects; organizes and displays items according to more complex system; bargains and trades with friends to obtain additional pieces.
- Names denominations of coins and paper money.
- Eager to save money and use for small purchases; develops simple plans for earning cash from odd jobs.
- Beginning to take an interest in what others think and do, for example, friends, different cultures, far away places.
- Plans ahead: "I'm saving this cookie for tonight."
- Fascinated with magic tricks; enjoys putting on "shows" for parents and friends.
- Uses more sophisticated logic in efforts to understand everyday events; for example, becoming systematic in looking for a misplaced jacket or toy.
- Can tell time; identifies the correct day, month, and year.
- Understands concepts of cause and effect, "a glass will break if dropped," "brushing helps to prevent cavities."
- Is learning addition and subtraction of numbers.
- Can effectively use words to express written or spoken thoughts.
- Letter reversals and sound substitution still common in some children.
- Recalls details from stories with considerable accuracy.
- Enjoys reading books and stories independently.

"The cat was this big!"

Speech and Language Development

- Enjoys storytelling; likes to write short stories, tell imaginative tales.
- Exaggerates the truth in many instances: "Teacher liked my picture the best," "I can eat a hundred hamburgers."
- Uses adult-like sentence structure and language in conversation; patterns reflect cultural and geographical differences.
- Uses gestures to illustrate conversations.
- Describes personal experiences in great detail: "First we parked the car, then we hiked up this long trail, then we sat down on a broken tree near a lake and ate...."
- Delights in telling jokes and riddles.
- Understands and carries out multiple step instructions (up to 5 steps); may need to have directions repeated because of not listening to entire request the first time.
- Enjoys writing simple letters to friends.
- Uses language to criticize and compliment others.

Personal-Social Development

- Plays with two or three close friends, usually of the same age and gender; also enjoys spending some time alone.
- Less critical of own performance, but is still easily frustrated and upset when unable to complete a task or when the product does not meet expectations.

Likes talking with friends on telephone

- Still blames others or makes up alibis to explain own shortcomings or mistakes.
- Enjoys talking with friends on the telephone.
- Becoming more outgoing; sees humor in everyday happenings; is cooperative and affectionate toward adults and less frequently annoyed with them.
- Less fearful: has fewer nightmares and is less afraid of the dark, parents dying, or of the home burning.
- Likes to be the "teacher's helper"; eager for teacher's attention and approval, but less obvious about seeking it.
- Interested in belonging to groups, cliques, talking in code; acceptance by peers is very important.
- Feelings easily hurt; may worry about not being liked; may cry, be embarrassed, or state adamantly "I will never play with you again" when criticized.
- Takes responsibilities seriously; can be trusted to carry out directions and commitments; worries about being late for school or not getting work done on time.
- Quick to "tattle" when others are not obeying rules or adhering to convention.

DAILY ROUTINES—SEVEN- AND EIGHT-YEAR-OLDS

Eating

- Most have a hearty appetite; boys typically eat more than girls. Those who have been picky eaters often show improved appetites.
- Eats most foods; has fewer likes and dislikes.
- Interested in foods; likes to help shop for and prepare meals.
- Takes pride in using good table manners, especially when eating out or when company is present; at home manners may be less than acceptable.
- Uses eating utensils with relative ease; seldom eats with fingers; some children still have trouble cutting meat.
- Often gulps food in order to return to play or a project in progress.

Bathing, Dressing, Toileting

- Has good control of bowel and bladder; can delay going to the bathroom without having an accident; may urinate more frequently when stressed.
- Establishes fairly regular pattern of elimination.
- Handwashing often hurried; dirt tends to go on towel rather than down the drain.
- May dillydally at bathtime; once in the tub seems to thoroughly enjoy the experience; can manage own bath without help.
- Takes greater interest in appearance, selecting and coordinating outfits, brushing hair, looking good.
- Dresses self; dawdling continues but child can speed up when time becomes critical.
- Beginning to take more interest in caring for own clothes; hangs clothes up (at least some of the time), helps with laundry, folds and returns items to dresser.
- Skilled at tying shoes, but often can't be bothered.

Often needs reminding about tying shoes

Sleeping

- Averages 10 hours of sleep at night; many children need less (may account for their efforts to delay bedtime).

- Begins to question established bedtime; wants to stay up later; dawdles, becomes sidetracked while getting ready for bed.

- Sleeps soundly, no longer bothered by bad dreams and nightmares.

- Often wakes up early, reads or occupies self in bed with toys or a simple activity: counting out savings in piggybank, looking at baseball card collection, reading.

May enjoy reading in bed.

Play and Social Activities

- Likes to join clubs and participate in organized group activities (Girl/Boy Scouts, Boys' and Girls' Clubs, swim teams).

Eager to join organized groups.

- Group membership becomes more important than the need for personal achievement.
- Enjoys competitive sports (soccer, baseball, swimming, gymnastics); eager to join a team; just as eager to quit if too much forced competition.
- Eager for acceptance from peers; beginning to imitate clothing styles, hairstyles, behavior, and language of most admired peers.
- May begin to act like a know-it-all toward the end of the eighth year; becomes argumentative with peers (and adults).
- Does not want to miss school or scheduled events; wants to "keep up."

LEARNING ACTIVITIES

Seven- and eight-year-olds.

Tips for parents and caregivers.

- Provide (and join in) games that require a moderate degree of strategy: checkers, dominoes, card games, Chinese checkers, magic sets, guessing games with fairly obvious answers.
- Gather materials for creating art projects, models, science experiments: pieces of wood, plastic, various weights and textures of cardboard and paper, beads, fabric, yarn.
- Provide a variety of books to read as well as stories on audio and video cassettes; make frequent trips to the library.
- Offer dress-up clothes and props for planning and staging group shows; attend the performances.
- Provide doll house, farm or zoo set, service station or airport, complete with small scale people, animals, and equipment.
- Invest in an inexpensive camera; encourage the child to experiment.
- Arrange for skill building in non-competitive activities: swimming, dance, tumbling, skating, skiing, musical instruments; this is a time of *trying out* a variety of interests, seldom is there a long-term commitment.

DEVELOPMENTAL ALERTS

Check with a health care provider or early childhood specialist if, by the eighth or ninth birthday, the child *does not*:

- Attend and concentrate on the task at hand; show longer periods of sitting quietly, listening, responding appropriately.

- Express ideas clearly and fluently.

- Handle stressful situations without undue emotional upset (excessive crying, sleeping or eating disturbances, withdrawal, frequent anxiety).

- Enjoy school and challenge of learning.

- Make friends, play with other children, or join in activities requiring motor skills such as throwing, catching, running or climbing.

- Assume responsibility for personal care, for example, dressing, bathing, feeding self.

- Make friends; play well with other children.

- Show improved motor skills.

THE ELEMENTARY SCHOOL YEARS

Between eight and twelve years of age, friendships become more enduring. The child develops a truly mutual understanding and respect for the other person. Ways of thinking about themselves, others, and the world in general changes dramatically. During this period, the child learns more abstract ways of thinking, gains greater understanding about cause and effect, begins to use genuine logic in figuring out how things work. The child also comprehends that things really are the same in spite of being used for alternative purposes or seen from a different perspective—a shovel can be used not only for digging, but for prying; a soup bowl can be traced around to draw a circle.

The stretch of years from eight or nine to adolescence is usually enjoyable and peaceful for all concerned. The child has adjusted to being at school for six or more hours each day. The stresses, strains and frustrations of learning to read, write, do basic arithmetic and follow directions are long forgotten. Changes in physical growth and development are quite different from child to child during this period. Girls in particular grow more rapidly. Research finds girls as young as 8 or 9 may already be experiencing some of the early hormonal changes associated with puberty.

And so, the era of childhood comes to an end. The first eight years or so have been given over to dramatic changes. There has been the wondrous evolvement from a small, helpless infant into an adult-like individual capable of complex and highly coordinated motor, cognitive, language and social behaviors.

REVIEW QUESTIONS

1. List three characteristics that describe the level of cognitive functioning typical of seven- and eight-year-olds.
    a.

    b.

    c.

2. List three perceptual skills that indicate a seven- or eight-year-old's readiness to begin reading.
    a.

    b.

    c.

3. List three reasonable expectations for a six-year-old in terms of home routines.
    a.

    b.

    c.

4. List three developmentally appropriate activities that a teacher might plan to expand the language skills of seven- and eight-year-olds.
    a.

    b.

    c.

TRUE OR FALSE

1. Most seven- and eight-year-olds are able to take care of their own personal needs—bathing, dressing, eating—without assistance.

2. Seven- and eight-year-olds become quite skilled at accepting another's point of view.

3. Playing with blocks, sand, water, and housekeeping activities should be eliminated from kindergarten curriculum.

4. Team membership is not a realistic expectation for the typical seven- or eight-year-old.

5. Six-, seven- and eight-year-olds show no concept of logical thinking.

6. Seven- and eight-year-olds have a good appetite and will usually eat most foods that are served.

7. Sex–role stereotyping disappears completely by age six.

8. A riddle book, soccer ball, and stamp collecting kit would make appropriate gifts for an eight-year-old.

MULTIPLE CHOICE. Select one or more correct answers from the lists below:

1. A seven- or eight-year-old can be expected to
   a. respect the privacy of others.
   b. take care of younger brothers or sisters in parents' absence.
   c. get themselves and younger siblings ready for school without adult help or supervision.

2. Grammatical irregularities
   a. are not uncommon in six-year-olds.
   b. are a sign of abnormality; normally developing seven- and eight-year-olds would never be heard to say, "The mouses falled into the water."
   c. should always be corrected and the child made to practice the correct form by repeating it at least ten times.

3. Six- seven- and eight-year-olds
   a. do a good bit of tattling and bossing.
   b. make lasting friendships.
   c. are seldom aggressive, either verbally or physically.

4. Which of the following is not typical behavior of a seven- or eight-year-old?
   a. assigning character names to friends and playing "Ninja turtles."
   b. imitating the behavior of another child in the group.
   c. shouting "I quit. You're stupid."
   d. organizing friends to help construct a 'spaceship' from a large cardboard box.

CHAPTER 8

Where to Seek Help for a Child

One of the most persistently asked questions is if a child is developing normally. It is a perplexing and difficult question, because of the range of normalcy and the great variation among children of the same general age. It is a question that requires thorough and on-going deliberation and investigation. At the same time, it is a question that must be answered quickly.

Developmental problems or delays, if they do exist, must receive immediate attention. Research indicates that early identification and intervention can lessen the seriousness of a problem. Early interventions can also reduce, or prevent, negative impact on other areas of development. Reliable screening programs for infants and young children from birth through age five are widely available. Furthermore, federal legislation and money are available to assist in locating and treating young children with developmental problems. The screening programs are often community sponsored or associated with public school systems.

Parents are usually the first to suspect a developmental problem or delay in their child. Those who do not are the exception. It is parents who become uneasy or fear that something is not quite right. Even so, they may not seek help immediately for a variety of reasons:

- Denial that the condition is anything to worry about
- Reluctance to openly acknowledge that a problem does exist
- Uncertainty about how to locate professional help
- Uneasiness about seeking advice for a problem that is difficult to clearly identify or describe
- Self-doubt arising from having been told there is really no problem—that the child will eventually "outgrow" it
- Confusion over conflicting information given by clinicians
- Timidness about pressuring for further consultation.

Consequently, the problem often does not go away; instead, it worsens. For this reason parents must always be encouraged to talk about any misgivings or doubts they have about their child's development. Health-care professionals,

**Signs of developmental problems
may be subtle.**

teachers, caregivers—all who work or have contact with young children—must listen and be responsive to any concern parents express, directly or indirectly.

CAUSE FOR CONCERN

Deciding if a developmental delay or irregularity is of concern is not always easy. Some problems are so obvious they can readily be identified: the child with Down syndrome is easily recognized because of unique physical characteristics. However, the basis for determining many other developmental problems is not always clear-cut. The signs may be so subtle, so difficult to pinpoint, that it is hard to clearly distinguish between children who definitely have a problem—the definite yes's—and those who definitely do not have a problem—the definite no's.

To determine if a delay or deviation is of real concern, several factors need to be considered:

- Children who exhibit signs of developmental problems in certain areas often continue to develop much like a normal child in other respects; such children present a confusing developmental profile.
- Great variation exists in the range of children's achievements within developmental areas; the rate of maturation is uneven and conditions in

the child's environment are continually changing. Both maturation and environment interact to exert a strong influence on every aspect of the child's development.

- Developmental delays or problems may not be immediately apparent. Many children learn to compensate for slight deficiencies, such as a mild to moderate vision or hearing loss. It is not until later, when the child is placed in structured and more demanding situations, as in a first-grade reading class, that these deficiencies become obvious.

At what point should a hunch or uncomfortable feeling about a child's development be cause for concern and action? Whenever parents feel uncertain about a child's developmental progress or lack of progress, they should seek help. Parents who are uneasy about their child need to discuss their concerns with an early childhood specialist or health care provider. Together they can determine if developmental screening is warranted. Certainly, a developmental delay or irregularity demands investigation whenever it interferes with a child's ability to participate in everyday activities. In addition, the frequent occurrence of constant repetition of a troublesome behavior is often a reliable sign that help should be sought. Seldom, though, is a single incidence of a questionable behavior cause for concern. However, a child's continuing reluctance to attempt a new skill or to fully acquire a developmental skill should be a concern. For example, a ten-month-old infant who tries to sit alone, but still must use hands for support may

A child's reluctance to attempt new skills or to fully acquire a developmental skill is cause for concern.

Noting and recording a child's behavior
reveals what is actually occurring.

or may not have a problem. However, clusters or groups of delays or developmental differences are always a warning sign: a ten-month-old infant who is not sitting without support or not smiling and babbling in response to others, almost surely is experiencing developmental difficulty. In either case, the need for developmental screening is indicated.

EVALUATING THE YOUNG CHILD

Several levels of information-gathering are involved in a comprehensive developmental evaluation. These include observation, screening, and diagnostic assessment. A combination of observation and screening techniques are useful for initial location and identification of individual children with possible delayed or abnormal development. Diagnostic assessment includes in-depth testing and careful interpretation of test results. Clinicians from various disciplines should participate in the diagnosis. It is their responsibility to provide detailed information about the problem areas and the specific nature of the child's problems. For example, a four-year-old child's delayed speech patterns may be noted during routine screening procedures. Subsequent diagnostic testing may pinpoint several other conditions: a moderate, bilateral hearing loss (loss of hearing in both ears), a severe malocclusion (an overbite), withdrawn behaviors. Poor production of many letter sounds and an expressive vocabulary typical of a two-and-one-half-year old may also be noted. These findings can the be translated into educational strategies and intervention procedures that will benefit the child's overall development.

The evaluation process always begins with careful and systematic observation. Noting and recording various aspects of a child's behavior enables the evaluator—parent, teacher, clinician—to focus on what is actually occurring. In other words, observations provide information about what the child can and cannot do. Observational data can be obtained by using simple checklists, frequency counts (how often behavior occurs), or short written descriptions (anecdotal notes) of what a child does in a particular situation. Direct observation often confirms or rules out impressions or suspicions regarding a child's abilities. For example, a child may not count to five when asked to do so. That same child, however, may be observed to spontaneously and correctly count objects while at play. A child thought to be hyperactive may be observed to sit quietly for 5 to 10 minute stretches when given interesting and challenging activities, thereby ruling out hyperactivity. (NOTE: The term hyperactive is greatly overused and misused; it should be avoided in describing any young child other than one who has been clinically diagnosed as hyperactive.)

Parents' observations are particularly valuable. They provide information and understanding that cannot be obtained from any other source. They also give insight into parents' attitudes, perceptions and expectations concerning their child. Involving parents in the observation phase of evaluation may also help to reduce their anxiety. Even more importantly, direct observation often points up unrecognized strengths and abilities in a child. When parents actually see their

Participating in a pure-tone audiometric test

child engaged in appropriate activities it may encourage them to focus more on the child's strengths and less exclusively on the child's shortcomings.

Screening procedures, together with care observation, are important first steps in identifying developmental delays or problems. Screening tests assess a child's present level of performance. They evaluate the child's current abilities, deviations, delays and impairments in all major areas of development: fine and gross motor, perceptual-cognitive, speech and language, and personal-social adjustment. A fairly comprehensive picture of the child can be obtained from a medical examination of the child, a health and development history completed by the child's parents (see Appendices 2, 3 and 4), a brief parent interview, and vision and hearing evaluations. If problem areas are identified during routine developmental screening, further diagnostic testing is indicated. It must be remembered that *screening tests do not constitute a diagnosis*. Furthermore, screening tests should not be used as a basis for planning an intervention program. In every case, more than one instrument must be used to ensure a clear and valid picture of the child's development. By using more than one type of test, the shortcomings or limitations in any single screening instrument are reduced.

Screening Instruments

Several criteria must be considered in selecting an appropriate screening instrument.

- Age of child
- Cultural background of the family
- Native language of the family and child
- Severity and nature of the child's developmental problem.

A number of comprehensive assessment instruments are available for use with young children; however, not all of them evaluate all developmental areas. Some instruments are criterion-referenced; that is, a child's performance is compared to certain predetermined standards. Criterion-referenced tests measure whether the child has mastered a given skill such as tying a bow, walking a balance beam, matching shapes and colors. Other screening tests are norm-referenced: the child's performance is compared to a "norm" or average performance of other children of the same age or sex. For example, the child can count a given number of pennies, identify letters of the alphabet, build a tower of 6 blocks.

A sample of screening instruments are listed below:

- Apgar Scale—determines the physical status of the newborn. It evaluates muscle tone, respiration, color, heartbeat and reflexes at one and five minutes after birth.

- Neonatal Behavior Assessment Scale (Brazelton) with Kansas Supplements—provides a general assessment of overall behavioral responses to various stimuli in the full-term infant up to 28 days of age.
- Bayley Scales of Infant Development—assesses development in children birth through 2 1/2 years.
- Brigance Diagnostic Inventory of Early Development—a criterion-based screening tool appropriate for assessing children 0–6 years; measures development in all major areas through observations of child's performance.
- Brigance K and 1 Screen for Kindergarten and First-Grade Children—samples development and skills in language, motor ability, perception, number comprehension, and body awareness in children 5–7 years.
- Social Skills Rating System (SSRS)—a standardized questionnaire for evaluating social and problem–solving behaviors in children age 3–18 years.
- Denver Developmental Screening Test (DDST)—used with children 1 month–6 years to assess motor, language, cognitive and personal-social development.
- Developmental Profile 11—utilizes interviewing procedures to assess major developmental achievements in children 0–9 years.
- Developmental Indicators of Learning (DIAL) revised—especially useful for identifying three- and four-year-old children at risk for developmental delay prior to kindergarten.

Vision screening is important for identifying problems.

Sound localization is useful for informal testing of the young child's hearing.

- Peabody Picture Vocabulary Test (PPVT)—useful for evaluating the receptive and expressive vocabularies of children 2 1/2–18 years.
- Learning Accomplishment Profile (LAP)—a screening tool for evaluating the developmental skills of handicapped and non-handicapped children 0–6 years.
- Home Observation for Measurement of the Environment (HOME)—an instrument for assessing the home environment and responsiveness of adult care providers to children 0–6 years.
- Denver Eye Screen Test (DEST)—an instrument for individualized vision screening of children six months and older.
- Snellen Illiterate E—a vision-screening device for identifying vision acuity and potential muscle imbalance of the eyes in children 2 1/2 and older.
- Pure Tone Audiometry—used to measure the responses of children 2 1/2–18 years to a range of auditory tones; is especially useful for identifying children with middle ear problems.
- Sound localization—child turns to locate a source of sound: bell, voice, stereo speakers. While not a formal screening instrument, it is an effective method for screening hearing abilities of children 12 months to 2 1/2 years.

Intelligence tests, such as the Wechsler Intelligence Scale for Children (WISC) and the Stanford-Binet Intelligence Scales, are sometimes administered to young children. The purpose of IQ tests is to attempt to determine a child's ability to process information. Scores received on an IQ test are compared to scores of other children of the same age. These tests try to measure how much the child knows, how well the child solves problems, and how quickly the child can perform a variety of cognitive tasks. IQ tests and the resulting scores must be used with caution, even skepticism, where young children are concerned.

The IQ scores of infants and preschool-age children *are not valid predictors* of future or even current intellectual performance. Even though intelligence is influenced to some unknown degree by heredity and maturation, measurement of intelligence is not a developmental issue; IQ tests do not measure the opportunities the child has had to learn nor the quality of those learning experiences.

In general, standardized IQ tests do not account for these factors. Therefore, the use of a single IQ test score to determine a child's cognitive or intellectual skills *must always be challenged.*

Testing Results
The increasing and widespread use of assessment screening programs is of great benefit in detecting possible developmental problems in young children. However, the screening process itself can sometimes have a negative effect on the outcome. Children's attention spans are short and vary considerably from day to day, or from task to task. Illness, fatigue, anxiety, lack of cooperation, irritability,

or restlessness can also have a negative effect on performance as can unfamiliarity with the adult who is administering a test. Poor performance may also result when young children are unaccustomed to an environment or testing site: Often they are capable of doing much better in a familiar setting. Consequently, *results derived from developmental screening assessments must be regarded with caution.* The following points are included to serve as reminders:

- Interpret and use test results with extreme caution. Avoid drawing hasty conclusions. Above all, do not formulate a diagnosis from limited information or a single test score. In analyzing screening results, recognize that developmental test results are strictly a measure of the child's *abilities at that given moment.* They may not be an accurate representation of the child's actual development or developmental potential. Only an *on-going* assessment can provide a complete picture of the child's developing skills and abilities.
- Recognize the dangers of labeling an individual child as learning disabled, mentally retarded, or behavior disordered, especially on the basis of a single screening. Labels are of little benefit. They can, and often do, have a negative affect on both expectations for the child and ways that parents, caregivers, and teachers respond to the child.
- *Question test scores.* Test results can be interpreted incorrectly. One test may suggest that a child has a developmental delay when actually there is nothing wrong. Such conclusions are called false-negatives. The opposite conclusion can also be reached. A child may have a problem that does not show up in the screening and so may be incorrectly identified as normal. This is a false-positive. The first situation leads to unnecessary anxiety and disappointment for the child's family, or even changes in the way they respond to their child. The latter situation—the false-positive—can lull a family into not seeking further help, and so the child's problem worsens. Both of these situations can be avoided with careful interpretation of testing that is thorough and appropriate.
- Results from screening tests *do not* constitute a diagnosis. Additional information must be collected and in-depth clinical testing must be completed before a diagnosis is given or confirmed. Even then, errors may occur in diagnosing developmental problems. There are many reasons for misdiagnosis, such as inconsistent and rapid changes in a child's growth and developmental achievements or changing environmental factors, such as divorce or a move.
- Failed items on a screening test do not dictate curriculum items or skills to be taught. The test skills are but single items representative of a broad range of skills to be expected in a given developmental area at an approximate age. A child who cannot stand on one foot for 5 seconds will not overcome a developmental problem by being taught to stand on one foot for a given time period.

- And once again, test results do not predict the child's developmental future. As stressed earlier, screening tests measure a child's abilities and achievements at the time of testing. In many cases, the results do not correlate with subsequent testing. There is always the need for ongoing assessment and for in-depth clinical diagnosis when screening tests indicate potential problems and delays.

In the elementary grades, achievement tests are administered regularly by most school districts. These tests are designed to measure how much the child has been learning in school about specific subject areas. On such tests, the child is assigned a percentile ranking, based on a comparison with other children of the same grade level. For example, a child in the 50th percentile in math is doing as well as 50% of the children in the same grade. Again, test scores should be backed up by teachers' observations of children and by collected samples (portfolios) of children's work.

In conclusion, careful observation and developmental screening are integral parts of a comprehensive assessment of the young child. Such evaluations provide information about the status of the child, but only at the time of testing. Information obtained from observation and screenings, when used as an on-going process and interpreted judiciously, makes an important contribution to the overall assessment of a child's developmental status.

REVIEW QUESTIONS

1. List three ways that a parent may indicate anxiety about a possible developmental problem in their child.
   a.

   b.

   c.

2. List three behaviors that might cause one to suspect a developmental problem in a young child.
   a.

   b.

   c.

3. List three ways of evaluating a child for a possible developmental disability.
   a.

b.

c.

4. List three major areas of development that can be assessed with the appropriate screening instrument.
   a.

   b.

   c.

5. List three infant screening instruments.
   a.

   b.

   c.

TRUE OR FALSE

1. Reliable screening programs for children, birth through eight, are not readily available.

2. It is always easy to tell the normally developing child from the child who is not developing normally.

3. Developmental problems always show up at birth or within the first few weeks of life.

4. Parents' observations of the child are of little value.

5. The Denver Developmental Screening Test (DDST) is used exclusively as a test of newborn abilities.

6. The results of IQ tests must always be viewed with caution and skepticism.

7. Effective diagnosis can be formulated on the basis of a single test score.

8. Screening tests measure a child's ability only at the time of testing.

9. Achievement test scores are often expressed in percentile ratings.

MULTIPLE CHOICE. Select one or more correct answers from the lists below.

1. Parents who fear something is wrong with their child
   a. can be depended upon to seek help immediately.
   b. may be uncertain about how to go about getting help.
   c. may not seek further help because they have been told by a professional to stop worrying, that the child will "outgrow" it.

2. It may be difficult even for professionals to identify developmental problems because
   a. a child with a problem may be quite normal in many ways.
   b. a child may have learned to compensate for a developmental problem (learned to work around it).
   c. the child cannot talk and tell the professional what is wrong.

3. In evaluating the young child, first-hand observation is important because
   a. observation reveals what the child can actually do under everyday conditions.
   b. observations confirm or rule out suspicious or casual impressions about the child.
   c. a child may show skills during an observation session not exhibited during a formal testing situation.

4. Screening instruments include those
   a. designed to give a specific IQ score.
   b. that measure only language performance.
   c. designed to assess the home environment including aspects of parent-child interactions.

5. Infant screening tests
   a. are always predictive of a child's future performance as a teenager.
   b. measure both reflexive and voluntary motor behaviors.
   c. can and should be done within the first few minutes of life.

6. Test scores
   a. always provide accurate assessment of the child's abilities and should never be questioned by parents or caregivers.
   b. often reflect how the child is feeling on a given day, rather than his or her best performance.
   c. are sufficient for formulating a complete diagnosis and treatment guide for children with developmental problems.

CHAPTER 9

Where to Go for Help

Referral and treatment are required when screening tests, assessments or other evaluations indicate the possibility of a developmental problem. Without immediate follow-up and intervention services, parents often feel helpless, confused, and anxious. They may even feel guilty about their child's problem. Children, in turn, may become equally confused and anxious because they sense subtle (or not so subtle) changes in their parents' expectations and attitudes.

THE DEVELOPMENTAL TEAM

Effective treatment of a developmental problem or delay requires the pooling of knowledge, in other words, a team approach. There must be collaboration among practitioners and agencies that specialize in serving young children and their families. A child's growth and development depends upon a balanced interrelatedness of the various developmental areas. A delay in one area invariably interferes with development in other areas, just as progress in one supports progress in others. If a three-year-old has a hearing loss, the child is likely to have problems with language, as well as with cognitive and social development. The ability to hear well is central to language development and language development is central to both cognitive and social development. The services of an audiologist, speech and language therapist, psychologist, early childhood teacher and, perhaps, a social-service agency, may all be required to provide adequate intervention services for this three-year-old child with a hearing impairment. Communication and cooperation among specialists and agencies providing services to young children is essential if the team approach is to benefit the child's overall development. Information must be shared, services coordinated and duplication avoided.

It is federal law that parents be involved in their child's assessment and intervention procedures. They have valuable information to contribute. In addition, many parents are able to learn and apply therapy recommendations at home. Sustained interest and participation in their child's intervention program is achieved if the developmental team abides by the following:

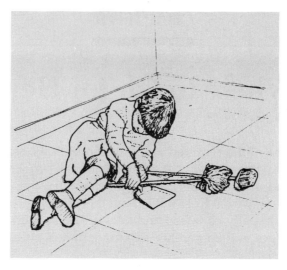

**Identifying the problem: This child has
cerebral palsy.**

- Keeps parents informed.
- Explains rationales for treatment procedures.
- Points out and emphasizes the child's progress.
- Teaches the parents ways of working with their child at home (if the parent is able to do so).
- Provides parents with positive feedback for their continued efforts on behalf of the child.

REFERRALS

The referral process first involves identifying the problem. The second step is to put parents and child in touch with educational programs and appropriate clinical services. Clinicians who may need to see the child might include a pediatrician, dentist, ophthamologist, perceptual-motor specialist, speech therapist and dietician.

Initially, the child's strengths, weaknesses and developmental needs are evaluated by the assessment team. The next step is to carefully match the child to services and educational programs available in the community. The family's financial resources and ability to provide transportation must also be taken into consideration. If a family cannot afford special services, has no knowledge of financial assistance programs and does not own a car, it is unlikely that the family

The classroom teacher and other members of
the developmental team conduct periodic
reviews of the child's progress.

can carry out recommendations for treatment. However, rarely are such problems insurmountable. Most communities have social-service agencies that can help families find and make use of needed services.

After an intervention program has been planned, a team coordinator, often called a case manager, works with the family. The case manager helps the family to establish initial contacts and set up arrangements with the recommended services and agencies. At this point, many parents become overwhelmed. They find the task of approaching multiple agencies and surmounting bureaucratic red tape more than they can manage. Many do not, or cannot, complete the arrangements unless they receive additional help. Therefore, a follow-up telephone call from the case manager is important. The call can remind and motivate parents to make final arrangements. Assistance can be given to parents with problems they may already have encountered. The need for a case manager is so crucial that it has been written into federal legislation (PL 99-457) designed to help families and young children with developmental problems.

Placing the child in an early childhood educational setting is frequently recommended by developmental teams. In such settings, classroom teachers and other members of the developmental team assume responsibility for conducting periodic reviews of the child's progress. The appropriateness of current placements and special services is evaluated on an on-going basis. In this way it can be determined whether the child's needs are being met. Throughout, there must be continuing communication and encouragement between teachers, practitioners and parents. Parents' understanding of the values of a program or special service are improved if one or both parents are contacted regularly. Frequent contacts also reinforce parents' cooperation and help to ensure that the intervention program is of maximum benefit to the child.

RESOURCES

Resources are available to families, caregivers, and teachers who work with children with (or at-risk for) developmental problems. These resources are provided at the local, state and national levels. They fall into two major categories: those that provide direct services and those that provide information.

Direct Services

Numerous agencies and organizations provide direct services and technical assistance. They help not only young children with developmental problems, but also their families and early childhood educators and caregivers working with such children. In addition, these agencies are a valuable referral source. Generally, they are aware of existing networks of services, agencies and qualified specialists. A sample of agencies and individuals who provide direct services to children follows.

- Public health departments at city, county or state levels
- Local public school systems, especially the special services division
- Hospitals and medical centers
- Well-child clinics

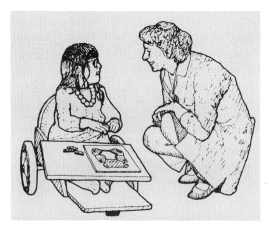

**Services for children with developmental problems
are available from a variety of agencies.**

- University affiliated services (UAF's)
- Head Start programs
- Mental health centers
- Child Find screening programs
- Early childhood centers and schools for exceptional children
- Practitioners from many disciplines: pediatricians, nurses, psychologists, audiologists, ophthamologists, educators, early-childhood specialists, speech and language therapists, occupational and physical therapists, social workers

Local service groups also are important resources. Many of these organizations provide specific types of services. These include financial assistance, transportation, location of necessary resources, and the purchase of special equipment.

A number of national organizations provide direct assistance to children and families with specific needs. These include:

- Parents of Down Syndrome Children
- American Foundation for the Blind
- Association for Children with Learning Disabilities
- United Cerebral Palsy Foundation
- National Society for Autistic Children
- International Parents Organization (Deaf)
- Epilepsy Foundation of America
- National Easter Seal Society for Crippled Children

Their current addresses can be found in most telephone books or through the local public library information services.

In addition, there are programs and agencies whose purpose is to give direct, technical assistance to educational programs and agencies serving young children with developmental problems. Many of these organizations also provide instructional materials. A sample of such agencies includes:

- National Information Center for Handicapped Children and Youth (NICHCY);
- Head Start Resource Access Projects (RAPs). Their purpose is to help Head Start programs provide comprehensive services to children with developmental problems;
- National Early Childhood-Technical Assistance System (NEC-TAS). This agency provides many kinds of assistance to federally funded handicapped children's projects;
- American Printing House for the Blind. This group produces a variety of materials and services for children with visual impairments. Materials

include talking books, magazines in braille, large-type books and other materials such as a textbook, *The Visually Impaired Child, Growth, Learning, Development: Infancy to School Age*, intended for educators of blind and visually impaired children.

A variety of support services and organizations also are available in most communities. These are designed to help families cope with the special challenges and demands of caring for a child with developmental problems. The stress level among these families is often great. A child's developmental problems affect every member of the family and cause inescapable adjustments in family lifestyles. However, many emotional and financial problems can be eased or avoided altogether if the family is given early assistance and support. Assistance can take the form of marriage counseling, financial management, **respite care**, mental-health counselling, medical care, or help with transportation, household chores, laundry, and child care.

Support groups are another service-oriented resource. They provide opportunities for parents to share their experiences with families having similar problems and concerns. Parents can be supported as they work toward strengthening their parenting skills. They can also be helped to learn and practice more effective ways to manage and discipline their child with special needs.

Information
A wide range of information is published for parents, caregivers, and professionals who work with children with developmental problems. Professional journals, government publications, and reference books are available in most public libraries. These can be readily located with the help of the librarian. Special interest groups and professional organizations also provide a wealth of printed materials focused on high-risk children and children with developmental delays. Only a few are listed here:

- Professional journals and periodicals, such as the *Journal of the Division for Early Childhood, Topics in Early Childhood Special Education, Exceptional Children*, and *Teaching Exceptional Children;*
- Trade magazines for parents such as *Parents of Exceptional Children* and *Parents Magazine;*
- Government documents, reports and pamphlets. These are available on almost any topic related to child development, child care, early intervention, parenting, and every type of developmental problem. Publications can be purchased through the Superintendent of Documents, U.S.

---

respite care—child care assistance given to families to allow them temporary relief from the demands of caring for a disabled child.

Government Printing Office, Washington, D.C., 20402; many are available in local government buildings.

- Bibliographic indexes and abstracts usually located in university, college and large public libraries. These are particularly useful to students and practitioners who need to locate quickly what is available on a specific topic. Two of many examples are the following:

  - *The Review of Child Development*
  - *Current Topics in Early Childhood Education.*

- Professional associations that focus on children's issues include:

  - Council for Exceptional Children (CEC), especially the Division for Early Childhood (DEC) within the Council;
  - National Association for the Education of Young Children (NAEYC);
  - National Association for Retarded Citizens (NARC);
  - American Association on Mental Deficiency (AAMD);
  - Children's Defense Fund;
  - American Speech, Language, and Hearing Association;
  - National Society for Autistic Children.

LEGISLATION

Several pieces of landmark legislation have been enacted on behalf of infants and young children during the last three decades. The goal of each is to reduce developmental problems through prevention, early identification, and early intervention programs. Major laws include;

- P.L. 88–452 (1965): This was part of the antipoverty reform of the 1960s. One section of this law provided for the establishment of Head Start and for supplemental services, such as developmental screening, medical and dental care, nutritious meals, and compensatory early education for young children living at or near the poverty level. Amendments to the law in 1972 and 1974 opened the doors of Head Start to children with disabilities. In 1990, the Head Start Expansion and Quality Improvement Act was passed as a part of P.L. 101–501. This law reauthorized Head Start through 1994, significantly increased federal monies to fund the program, and allows for opportunities for collaboration between the new Head Start disability regulation and IDEA, Part B.
- The National Program for Early and Periodic Screening, Diagnosis and Treatment (EPSDT) (1967): This program is designed to evaluate children at developmental risk from a physical and psychological perspective, and also to address the needs of the family.

- Supplemental Feeding Program for Women, Infants and Children (WIC) (1972): This law created a medically prescribed nutrition program designed to improve maternal health during pregnancy, to promote full-term prenatal development and to increase birth weight of newborns. It is also aimed at improving the general health of infants and young children who receive inadequate nutrition, which puts them at risk for developmental problems.
- P.L. 94–142 (1975): Originally called the Education for All Handicapped Children Act (EHA), this was renamed the Individuals with Disabilities Education Act (IDEA) (P.L. 101–476) in 1990. A major intent was to motivate the states to provide comprehensive prevention, treatment, and individualized educational programs (IEP) for children with developmental problems and those at developmental risk.
- P.L. 99–457 (1986): This was a major amendment to P.L. 94–142. Reauthorized in 1990 as P.L. 102–119, this law makes specific and comprehensive provisions for children with developmental problems, and for their families as well, through the Individualized Family Service Plan (IFSP). Currently, all states are in compliance: free and appropriate educational programs are on record as being available to all three to five-year-old children with developmental problems. The act also provides funds for states that choose to serve infants and toddlers who have or are at risk for, developmental problems. By mid-1993, all states and several territories had chosen to apply for funds.
- P.L. 101–336 (1990): Titled the Americans With Disabilities Act, this is a national civil rights law that protects against discrimination based on a person's disability. The major intent is to remove barriers that interfere with full inclusion in every aspect of society—education, employment, public services. Implications for young children and their families are clear; by law, preschool and child care programs must adapt their settings to accommodate children with disabilities.

In conclusion, finding help for children with developmental problems is not a simple matter. The issue is complex; some children present tangles of interrelated developmental problems. These problems seem to multiply during the crucial first five years of a child's life if not dealt with as early as possible. Effective intervention must be comprehensive, integrated, and on-going. In addition, it must be directed toward several developmental areas at the same time. This requires team work on the part of specialists from many disciplines, agencies and organizations working cooperatively with the child and family. It also requires that everyone involved with the child be aware of the available resources and know how to tie in with them. Everyone involved must have a working knowledge of the legislative acts that help to provide services for children with developmental problems and their families.

REVIEW QUESTIONS

1. List three of the several professions that routinely serve on a developmental team.

    a.

    b.

    c.

2. List three responsibilities of a developmental team.

    a.

    b.

    c.

3. List three sources of direct, hands-on services for a child and family with developmental problems.

    a.

    b.

    c.

4. List three organizations that focus solely on specific handicapping or disabling conditions.

    a.

    b.

    c.

5. List three pieces of federal legislation enacted since 1970 that serve young children who are at-risk for, or have, a handicapping condition.

    a.

    b.

    c.

TRUE OR FALSE

1. Parents never feel guilty about their child's problems, especially when they could not possibly have caused it.

2. A delay or problem in one developmental area almost always affects other developmental areas.

3. Because of the high costs, there is no clinical help available for a disabled child if a parent is out of work or living at the poverty level.

4. Case managers are an unnecessary expenditure, even a luxury, on a developmental team.

5. There are few government documents or publications suitable for use by parents, caregivers or teachers.

6. WIC is a federal program aimed at helping unskilled mothers learn a self-supporting job skill.

7. Effective intervention must be concerned with all areas of development simultaneously.

8. Child Find programs are aimed at locating missing children.

9. Placement in early childhood educational programs is a frequent recommendation of a developmental child-study team.

10. Parents have no role in screening or intervention procedures until the professionals have completed their work-up and inform parents of the results.

MULTIPLE CHOICE. Select one or more correct answers from the lists below.

1. If a young child has an undetected hearing loss that child is likely to have additional problems with
    a. language development.
    b. social development.
    c. cognitive development.

2. The following organizations provide assistance to disabled children and their families
   a. National Society for Autistic Children
   b. Audobon Society
   c. Epilepsy Foundation of America

3. The role of the case manager is to
   a. assist parents through the team process.
   b. keep parents informed of each step the team takes on behalf of the child.
   c. reprimand parents when they fail to keep records or appointments with the team members.

4. The referral process includes
   a. identification of a child's problem.
   b. decisions as to which professionals should see the child.
   c. helping find transportation for those families who cannot find it for themselves.

5. P.L. 99–457 mandates
   a. an individual service plan for the family as a whole.
   b. federal money for setting up early identification and intervention programs within each state.
   c. stiff fines (even imprisonment) for parents or teachers who do not report a disabling condition to the proper authorities.

Summary of Reflexes

Age	Appears	Disappears
birth	swallow*, gag*, cough*, yawn*, blind* suck rooting startle Moro grasp stepping plantar elimination Tonic neck reflex (TNR)	
1–4 months	Landau tear* (cries with tears)	grasp suck (becomes voluntary) step root Tonic neck reflex (TNR)
4–8 months	parachute palmar grasp pincer grasp	
8–12 months		Moro palmar grasp plantar reflex
12–18 months		
18–24 months		Landau
3–4 years		parachute elimination (becomes voluntary)

*Permanent; present throughout person's lifetime.

Developmental Checklists

A simple checklist, one for each child, is a useful observation tool for anyone working with infants and young children. The questions on the checklists that follow can be answered in the course of a child's everyday activities over a period of a week or more. "No" answers signal that a problem may exist and further investigation is probably a good idea. Several "no" answers indicate that additional investigation is a necessity.

The "sometimes" category is also an important one. It suggests what the child can do, at least part of the time, or under some circumstances. The "sometimes" category provides space where brief notes and comments can be recorded about how and when a behavior occurs. What the child may need is more practice, incentive, or adult encouragement. Hunches often provide a good starting point for working with the child. Again if "sometimes" is checked a number of times, further investigation is in order.

The observation checklists may be duplicated and used as part of the assessment process. A completed checklist contains information about a child that members of a developmental team would find useful in evaluating a child's development status and in determining an intervention program.

Child's Name _____ Age _____

Observer _____ Date _____

DEVELOPMENTAL CHECKLIST

BY 12 MONTHS: Does the Child	Yes	No	Sometimes
Walk with assistance?			
Roll a ball in imitation of an adult?			
Pick objects up with thumb and forefinger?			
Transfer objects from one hand to other hand?			
Pick up dropped toys?			
Look directly at adult's face?			
Imitate gestures: peek-a-boo, bye-bye, pat-a-cake?			
Find object hidden under a cup?			
Feed self crackers (munching, not sucking on them)?			
Hold cup with two hands; drink with assistance?			
Smile spontaneously?			
Pay attention to own name?			
Respond to "no"?			
Respond differently to strangers and familiar persons?			
Respond differently to sounds: vacuum, phone, door?			
Look at person who speaks to him or her?			
Respond to simple directions accompanied by gestures?			
Make several consonant-vowel combination sounds?			
Vocalize back to person who has talked to him or her?			
Use intonation patterns that sound like scolding, asking, exclaiming?			
Say "da-da" or "ma-ma"?			

Child's Name _____ Age _____

Observer _____ Date _____

DEVELOPMENTAL CHECKLIST

BY TWO YEARS: Does the Child	Yes	No	Sometimes
Walk alone?			
Bend over and pick up toy without falling over?			
Seat self in child-size chair? Walk up and down stairs with assistance?			
Place several rings on a stick?			
Place 5 pegs in a peg board?			
Turn pages 2 or 3 at a time?			
Scribble?			
Follow one-step direction involving something familiar: "Give me—." "Show me—." "Get a —."			
Match familiar objects?			
Use spoon with some spilling?			
Drink from cup holding it with one hand, unassisted?			
Chew food?			
Take off coat, shoe, sock?			
Zip and unzip large zipper?			
Recognize self in mirror or picture?			
Refer to self by name?			
Imitate adult behaviors in play—for example, feeds "baby"?			
Help put things away?			
Respond to specific words by showing what was named: toy, pet, family member?			
Ask for desired items by name: (cookie)?			
Answer with name of object when asked "What's that"?			
Make some two word statements: "Daddy bye-bye"?			

Child's Name _____ Age _____

Observer _____ Date _____

DEVELOPMENTAL CHECKLIST

BY THREE YEARS: Does the Child	Yes	No	Sometimes
Run well in a forward direction?			
Jump in place, two feet together?			
Walk on tiptoe?			
Throw ball (but without direction or aim)? Kick ball forward?			
String 4 large beads?			
Turn pages in book singly?			
Hold crayon: imitate circular, vertical, horizontal strokes?			
Match shapes?			
Demonstrate number concepts of one and two? (Can select one or two; can tell if one or two objects.)			
Use spoon without spilling?			
Drink from a straw?			
Put on and take off coat?			
Wash and dry hands with some assistance?			
Watch other children; play near them; sometimes join in their play?			
Defend own possessions?			
Use symbols in play—for example, tin pan on head becomes helmet and crate becomes a space ship.			
Respond to "Put—in the box," "Take the—out of the box"?			
Select correct item on request: big vs little; one vs two?			
Identify objects by their use: show own shoe when asked, "What do you wear on your feet?"			
Ask questions?			
Tell about something with functional phrases that carry meaning: "Daddy go airplane." Me hungry now"?			

Child's Name _____ Age _____

Observer _____ Date _____

DEVELOPMENTAL CHECKLIST

BY FOUR YEARS: Does the Child	Yes	No	Sometimes
Walk on a line?			
Balance on one foot briefly? Hop on one foot?			
Jump over an object 6 inches high and land on both feet together?			
Throw ball with direction?			
Copy circles and crosses?			
Match 6 colors?			
Count to 5?			
Pour well from pitcher? Spread butter, jam with knife?			
Button, unbutton large buttons?			
Know own sex, age, last name?			
Use toilet independently and reliably?			
Wash and dry hands unassisted?			
Listen to stories for at least 5 minutes?			
Draw head of person and at least one other body part?			
Play with other children?			
Share, take turns (with some assistance)?			
Engage in dramatic and pretend play?			
Respond appropriately to "Put it beside," "Put it under"?			
Responds to two step directions: "Give me the sweater and put the shoe on the floor"?			
Respond by selecting the correct object—for example, hard vs. soft object?			
Answer "if," "what," and "when" questions?			
Answer questions about function: "What are books for"?			

Child's Name _____ Age _____

Observer _____ Date _____

DEVELOPMENTAL CHECKLIST

BY FIVE YEARS: Does the Child	Yes	No	Sometimes
Walk backward, heel to toe?			
Walk up and down stairs, alternating feet?			
Cut on line?			
Print some letters?			
Point to and name 3 shapes?			
Group common related objects: shoe, sock and foot: apple, orange and plum?			
Demonstrate number concepts to 4 or 5?			
Cut food with a knife: celery, sandwich?			
Lace shoes?			
Read from story picture book—in other words, tell story by looking at pictures?			
Draw a person with 3 to 6 body parts?			
Play and interact with other children; engage in dramatic play that is close to reality?			
Build complex structures with blocks or other building materials?			
Respond to simple three step directions: "Give me the pencil, put the book on the table, and hold the comb in your hand"?			
Respond correctly when asked to show penny, nickel, and dime?			
Ask "How" questions?			
Respond verbally to "Hi" and "How are you"?			
Tell about event using past and future tense?			
Use conjunctions to string words and phrases together—for example, "I saw a bear and a zebra and a giraffe at the zoo"?			

Child's Name _____ Age _____

Observer _____ Date _____

DEVELOPMENTAL CHECKLIST

BY SIX YEARS: Does the Child	Yes	No	Sometimes
Walk across a balance beam?			
Skip with alternating feet?			
Hop for several seconds on one foot?			
Cut out simple shapes?			
Copy own first name?			
Show well-established handedness; demonstrate consistent right or left handedness?			
Sort objects on one or more dimensions: color, shape or function?			
Name most letters and numerals?			
Count by rote to 10; know what number comes next?			
Dress self completely; tie bows?			
Brush teeth unassisted?			
Have some concept of clock time in relation to daily schedule?			
Cross street safely?			
Draw a person with head, trunk, legs, arms and features; often add clothing details?			
Play simple board games?			
Engage in cooperative play with other children, involving group decisions, role assignments, rule observance?			
Use construction toys, such as Leggos, blocks, to make recognizable structures?			
Do 15 piece puzzles?			
Use all grammatical structures: pronouns, plurals, verb tenses, conjunctions?			
Use complex sentences: carry on conversations?			

Child's Name _____ Age _____

Observer _____ Date _____

DEVELOPMENTAL CHECKLIST

BY SEVEN YEARS: Does the Child	Yes	No	Sometimes
Concentrate on completing puzzles and board games?			
Ask many questions?			
Use correct verb tenses, word order, and sentence structure in conversation?			
Correctly identify right and left hands?			
Make friends easily?			
Show some control of anger, using words instead of physical aggression?			
Participate in play that requires teamwork and rule observance?			
Seek adult approval for efforts?			
Enjoy reading and being read to?			
Use pencil to write words and numbers?			
Sleep undisturbed through the night?			
Catch a tennis ball, walk across balance beam, hit ball with bat?			
Plan and carry out simple projects with minimal adult help?			
Tie own shoes?			
Draw pictures with greater detail and sense of proportion?			
Care for own personal needs with some adult supervision? Wash hands? Brush teeth? Use toilet? Dress self?			
Show some understanding of cause-and-effect concepts?			

Child's Name _____ Age _____

Observer _____ Date _____

DEVELOPMENTAL CHECKLIST

BY EIGHT AND NINE YEARS: Does the Child	Yes	No	Sometimes
Have energy to play, continuing growth, few illnesses?			
Use pencil in a deliberate and controlled manner?			
Express relatively complex thoughts in a clear and logical fashion?			
Carry out multiple (4–5) step instructions?			
Become less easily frustrated with own performance.			
Interact and play cooperatively with other children			
Show interest in creative expression—telling stories, jokes, writing, drawing, singing?			
Use eating utensils with ease?			
Have a good appetite? Show interest in trying new foods?			
Know how to tell time?			
Have control of bowel and bladder functions?			
Participate in some group activities—games, sports, plays?			
Want to go to school? Seem disappointed if must miss a day?			
Demonstrate beginning skills in reading, writing, and math?			

Child Health History

SAMPLE FORM

We appreciate your taking time to fill out this form as completely as possible. The information will be treated in a confidential manner and used for evaluating and for planning your child's program.

GENERAL INFORMATION

1. Child's Name _____ , _____.
   (First)   (Last)

2. Child's Address _____.
   (Street)

   _____
   (City, State, Zip)

3. Home Telephone Number____(   )_____.

4. Child's Sex: _____ Female   _____ Male

5. Child's Date of Birth_____ _____ _____
   Month   Date   Year

6. Mother's Name_____.

7. Father's Name_____.

BIRTH HISTORY

8. Length of Pregnancy: _____ 6 _____ 7 _____ 8 _____ 9 months

9. Child's weight at birth: _____ lbs. _____ ozs. or _____ kilograms

10. _____ yes _____ no Were there any unusual factors or complications during this pregnancy? Please describe.

   _____.

11. Did your child have any medical problems at the time of birth—for example, jaundice, difficulty breathing, birth defects? Please describe:_____

   _____.

12. What doctor is most familiar with your child? _____.

   Doctor's telephone number: _____

13. Does your child take any medications on a regular basis? __yes __ no If yes, name of medication and dosage: _____.

14. Has your child had any of the following illnesses (dates)?

   _____ measles   _____ rheumatic fever

   _____ mumps   _____ chicken pox

   _____ whooping cough   _____ pneumonia

   _____ middle ear infection   _____ hepatitis
         (otitis media)

   _____ meningitis

15. Where there any sick complications with these illnesses, such as high fever, convulsions, muscle weaknesses, and so on. Please describe: _____

   _____.

16. _____ yes _____ no Has your child ever been hospitalized? _____ Number of times _____ Total length of time.

   Reasons:_____

17. _____ yes _____ no Has your child had any other serious illness or injuries that did not involve hospitalization?

18. How many colds has your child had during the past year?

19. Does your child have:

    ____ yes ____ no Allergies? To (please specify)

       Foods _____

       Animals _____

       Medicine _____

    ____ yes ____ no Asthma?

    ____ yes ____ no Hayfever?

20. ____ yes ____ no Has your child had any problems with earaches or ear infections? If YES, how often in the past year? _____

21. ____ yes ____ no Has your child's hearing been tested?

    When _____ _____ Was there any evidence of hearing loss
           (month)   (year)
    (describe)? _____.

22. ____ yes ____ no Does your child currently have tubes in his or her ears?

23. Do you have any concerns about your child's speech or language development?

    ____ yes ____ no If YES, describe: _____.

24. ____ yes ____ no Has your child's vision been tested?

    Date of test: _____ month _____ year

25. ____ yes ____ no Was there any evidence of vision loss?

    Please describe: _____.

26. Does your child do some things that you find troublesome?

    Please describe: _____.

27. Has your child ever participated in out-of-the-home child care services—for example, sitter, day care, preschool? Describe: _____.

CHILD'S PLAY ACTIVITIES

28. Where does your child usually play—for example, backyard, kitchen, bedroom?

    _____.

29. Does your child usually play: _____ alone? _____ with 1–2 other children? _____ with brothers/sisters?

    _____ with older children? _____ with younger children?

    _____ with children of the same age?

30. Is your child usually _____ cooperative? _____ shy? _____ aggressive?

31. What are some of your child's favorite toys and activities?

    Please describe: _____.

32. Are there any particular behaviors you would like us to watch?

    Describe:_____.

CHILD'S DAILY ROUTINE

33. Do you have any concerns about your child's:

    _____ eating habits?

    _____ sleeping habits?

    _____ toilet training?

    If YES, please describe: _____.

34. ____ yes ____ no Is your child toilet trained. If YES, how often does your child have an accident? _____.

35. What word(s) does your child use or understand for:

    urination _____ bowel movement_____

36. How many hours does your child sleep? At night _____ ?

    Goes to bed at: _____ p.m. Awakens at: _____ a.m.

    Afternoon nap: _____.

37. When your child is upset, how do you comfort him or her?

    _____.

38. The term "family" has many different meanings. Since the topic of families and family members is often included in classroom discussions, please list or describe who your child considers to be "family" at home. _____

    _____.

39. How many brothers and (or) sisters does your child have?
    Brothers: (ages)   Sisters: (ages)

    _____   _____

    _____   _____

    _____   _____

40. What language(s) is/(are) most commonly spoken in your home?

    English _____ Other _____.

APPENDIX 4

Annotated Bibliography

CHILD DEVELOPMENT

Barclay, L. (1985). *Infant development*. New York: Holt, Rinehart, and Winston.
A comprehensive overview of child development from conception into the second year. Includes traditional developmental perspectives and research on issues such as the effects of child care and parenting practices.

Berns, R. (1994). *Topical child development*. Albany, NY: Delmar Publishers Inc.
Written by a sensitive child developmentalist, this is a text that combines psychological theory and research in ways that are delightfully descriptive and readily applicable to the lives of children in a topical approach.

Bentzen, M. (1993). *Seeing young children: a guide to observing and recording behavior (2nd Edition)*. Albany, NY: Delmar Publishers Inc.
A practical book on observing young children, recording their developmental progress, and using the information to foster each child's development.

Bjorklund, D. and Bjorklund, B. (1992). *Looking at children*. Pacific Groves, CA: Brooks/Cole Publishing Company.
An introductory text for practitioners that skillfully blends theory and research with practical application in language that is clear and understandable.

Charlesworth, R. (1992). *Understanding child development*. Albany, NY: Delmar Publishers Inc.
An excellent book for teachers, caregivers, and parents; the focus is on growth and development in the infant, toddler, and preschool child. A wealth of basic information is skillfully combined with numerous suggestions for working with young children.

Copeland, M.E. and Kimmel, J.R. (1989). *Evaluation and management of infants and young children with developmental disabilities*. Baltimore, MD: Paul H. Brooks.
An in-depth resource for developing successful interactions between children and their caregivers; includes specific sections on everyday living skills such as toileting, dressing, and feeding.

Flavell, J. H. (1985). *Cognitive development*. Englewood Cliffs, NJ: Prentice Hall.
No text on cognitive development can completely escape technical complexity, but this one, written by a leading researcher on cognitive develop-

ment and developmental theory, is one of the best, yet least difficult, because of its easy, anecdotal style.

Kopp, C. (1993). *Baby steps: the "why's" of your child's behavior in the first two years.* New York: W. H. Freeman Company.

Based on contemporary research, this book provides a step-by-step description of infant and toddler development in the social, cognitive, emotional, motor, and perceptual domains.

Santrock, J.W. (1994). *Children.* Dubuque, IA: Wm. C. Brown Publishers.

An appealing and easily read textbook that addresses contemporary topics in child development in a culturally sensitive manner. Extensive research findings, with emphasis on everyday application, are incorporated throughout the book.

CHILDREN WITH DEVELOPMENTAL PROBLEMS: IDENTIFICATION AND INTERVENTION

Allen, K. Eileen. (1993). *The exceptional child: Mainstreaming in early childhood education.* Albany, NY: Delmar Publishers Inc.

A comprehensive text based on developmental principles as they are applied to the inclusion and appropriate education of children of all developmental capabilities in early childhood programs.

Blackman, J.A. (1989). *Medical aspects of developmental disabilities in children birth through three.* Rockville, MD: Aspen Systems.

A highly recommended book for early childhood personnel; it provides well-illustrated and readily understood information about medical issues that affect the developmental progress of young children.

Hanson M. and Harris, S. (1986). *Teaching the young child with motor delays.* Austin, TX: Pro-Ed Publishers.

An easy-to-read book bridging the gap between parents and clinicians working with children, birth to three, with motor impairments; includes teaching strategies and therapy activities that can be used in the home and child care programs.

Krajicek, M. and Tomlinson, A. (1983). *Detection of developmental problems in young children.* Baltimore, MD: University Park Press.

Practical and readable, this is a highly acclaimed nursing text that focuses on screening, early identification, and beginning intervention strategies with children with potential or identified developmental problems.

McCormick, L. and Schiefelbusch, R. (1994). *Early language intervention.* Columbus, OH: Charles E. Merrill.

An excellent introduction to both normal and atypical language development; includes practical examples of programs, procedures, and materials for enhancing communication skills in young children.

Noonan, M.J. and McCormick, L. (1993). *Early intervention in natural environments*. Pacific Grove, CA: Brooks/Cole Publishing Co.

> A superior text that responds to the federal mandate to serve infants and young children with developmental problems in the natural environment of the family's choice, using play and other developmentally appropriate activities and learning opportunities.

Peterson, N. (1994). *Early intervention for handicapped and other at-risk children*. Denver, CO: Love Publishing Company.

> A beautifully complete text for students, professionals, and ancillary personnel working in early childhood inclusionary programs. The author provides an invaluable perspective on early intervention.

PARENTING

A reader's guide for parents of children with mental, physical or emotional disabilities. (1990). Woodbine House Publishers.

> An excellent collection of more than 1000 books and other resources about disabilities for parents of children with special needs. In addition to extensive subject and title indexes, this book also includes listings of organizations, parent advocacy groups, and professional agencies.

Beer, W. R. (1992). *American stepfamilies*. New Brunswick, NJ: Transaction Publishers.

> The author presents an overview of special concerns that face stepfamilies, particularly adult relationships and parent-child interactions. Extensive use of case histories and personal experiences lend a unique and sensitive insight into an often misunderstood family pattern.

Brooks, J.B. (1991). *The process of parenting*. Mountain View, Toronto, Canada: Mayfield Publishing Co.

> A comprehensive book that addresses many contemporary parenting issues. Information on behavior management and developmentally appropriate expectations are included for children at all stages along the developmental continuum. Special attention is also given to issues of working parents, the single parent, stepparenting, and children with specific needs.

Cataldo, C. (1987). *Parent education for early childhood*. NY: Teachers College Press.

> This is a particularly useful resource book for persons who are involved in parent education programs. It includes valuable information about establishing programs, staff training in parent education, participant recruitment, an overview of family patterns, and parent needs. The author stresses techniques that support parental efforts and promote children's growth and development.

Christophersen, E.R. (1988). *Little people: guidelines for common sense child rearing.* Kansas City, KS: Westport Publishers, Inc.
    A frank and witty presentation of management techniques, based on extensive research and experience in pediatric training programs, for common behavioral problems in young children.
Hamner, T. and Turner, P. (1990). *Parenting in contemporary society.* Englewood Cliffs, NJ: Prentice Hall.
    Examines the diversity of traditional and non-traditional family patterns in the U.S., along with cultural differences, socio-economic variations, working families, high-risk families, adoption and foster care, as well as families of exceptional children. Throughout this book, emphasis is placed on effective parenting strategies.
Jaffe, M.L. (1991). *Understanding parenting.* NY: Wm. C. Brown, Publishers.
    A review focus is on child-rearing problems that typically confront parents and caregivers of young children through adolescents. The importance of good parent-child relationships and communication is stressed throughout the text.
Marotz, L., Cross, M., and Rush, J. (1993). *Health, safety, and nutrition for the young child.* Albany, NY: Delmar Publishers Inc.
    A comprehensive overview of the numerous factors that enhance children's growth and development. It includes some of the most current research information and knowledge concerning each of these areas, and is especially useful for parents and caregivers.
Parenting: an ecological perspective. (1993). T. Luster and L. Okagaki (eds.). Hillsdale, NJ: Lawrence Erlbaum Associates, Publishers.
    An up-to-date compilation of research findings on a variety of contemporary issues related to differences in parenting behavior. These multidisciplinary studies were undertaken in an effort to improve the understanding of parental behavior and how to effectively enhance parent-child relationships.
Weiser, M. (1991). *Infant/toddler care and education.* NY: Macmillan Publishing Co.
    Another comprehensive book that focuses on the major aspects of care and educational approaches unique to the infant and toddler. This book is designed for parents and caregivers of children under three years of age.
Wilson, L.C. (1990). *Infants and toddlers.* Albany, NY: Delmar Publishers Inc.
    Parents and caregivers will find this book particularly useful in understanding developmental sequences, creating enriching environments and providing appropriate learning experiences for infants and toddlers based on their developmental needs.

Index